CRISIS COUNSELING

Other Continuum books by Eugene Kennedy

On Becoming A Counselor
Sexual Counseling
St. Patrick's Day with Mayor Daley and Other
Things Too Good to Miss

CRISIS COUNSELING

An Essential Guide
for Nonprofessional Counselors

EUGENE KENNEDY

CONTINUUM · NEW YORK

For
Monsignor Edward C. Herr
who, appearing at the time of a crisis,
would make everybody feel better.

1981
The Continuum Publishing Corporation
18 East 41st Street, New York, N.Y. 10017

Printed in the United States of America

Library of Congress Cataloging in Publication Data

Kennedy, Eugene C
   Crisis counseling.

   Bibliography: p.
   1. Crisis intervention (Psychiatry) 2. Counseling.
I. Title.
RC480.6.K46   616.89'025   80-27200
ISBN 0-8264-0038-8

Contents

I am particularly grateful to Michael McCauley of the Thomas More Association, who edited these materials when they appeared, in slightly different form, in a newsletter published by that organization. I am grateful as well to other editors there for their encouragement and for their suggestions about topics that deserved treatment.

Introduction

Whenever I stand up to speak before a group I always survey their faces, each grave with knowledge of life, and think to myself, "Nobody knows the trouble they've seen." Any random gathering, whether of people waiting for the bus to come or the show to begin, possesses the power to evoke a similar reaction in us because we are brother and sister to its members. Beyond our posturings, we know that daily existence is compounded of stresses and crises, and that there is no immunity from them for any of us.

Such a realization need not, of course, make us melancholy. Our passage takes place on a pitching deck, and sometimes the only thing we can do is hold on until the seas grow calm again. Only half-jokingly, men and women speak of living from one crisis to another, and Murphy's Law has become part of our folklore because it embodies a truth that we all recognize. Life may be defined as that experience in which things go wrong, and living may be understood as doing the best we can in these uncertain circumstances. We are parties to a crisis, our own or someone else's, every day.

Since we, along with the rest of this world, fall short of perfection, we often feel unprepared to handle effectively the emergencies that come into our lives. Expert help may be obtained only after some delay, and untrained persons from a wide variety of professions stand on the embattled front lines of crisis engagements. Pastors, teachers, doctors, lawyers, and others must respond when the emergency explodes, whether they are prepared to do so or not.

This is the final book in a trilogy of books written for such nonprofessional men and women. The first, *On Becoming A Counselor,* dealt with the general principles of counseling. While the second found its focus expressed in its title, *Sexual Counseling*. This work, while not a hand-book that indicates everything that should be done in critical moments, is a compendium of common sense, supported by the research that has been done in the specialized field of crisis management. These essays can only supplement healthy human instincts, which, in the long run, are the essential ingredients in responding to any serious emergency situation. When preparing a book for nonprofessional counselors, one must recognize that they have to handle acutely difficult problems in the course of almost every day of their work. This volume is designed to help such workers to respond more effectively and more confidently in their customary contacts with patients, students, or parishioners.

Some people cannot, of course, live without a crisis. If none exists, they find a way to cause at least the appearance of one. Such bearers of hysteria are found everywhere, but they are seldom of any lasting assistance to persons afflicted with intensely pressing problems. Perhaps the best crisis counselors are those who have a natural reluctance for this work—a certain diffidence mixed with a willingness to help—and who do not depend on emergencies to stimulate their own emotional lives. This book is not for those who need the excitement of crises for their own internal well-being. It is offered as a source of support for nonprofessional counselors who have troubles enough of their own and who do not need to borrow or invent any further complications in their lives. Because they understand that life is hazardous and that we are all, to use a governmental designation about research populations, "subjects at risk," such workers are able to reach out sensibly and sensitively during the raw and unprocessed moments of shock and dismay that flow like electric current from every serious crisis.

One can say of pastors, teachers, lawyers, physicians, and scores of others, that nobody knows the troubles they have seen either. We are all in their debt for the way they give of themselves daily to help the rest of us make our way through the critical events of our lives. May this work assist and encourage them as they continue to do so.

ONE

Is Life a Crisis?

Busy professionals find, as Lewis Mumford once observed, that the human condition is "always desperate." They need not be professionals in psychology or other mental health specialties to find that each day provides a harvest of crises, some great and some small, but each possessed of many similar characteristics. And one hardly surmounts or works through one emergency situation when another rudely shoulders its way into the environment. This happens in law offices, rectory parlors, plants and factories, and even in what seem to be the placid confines of sanitariums and monasteries. Things and people break down, at least temporarily, all the time; and the whole purpose of crisis counseling, no matter who the counselor is, is to get them going again.

If Humpty Dumpty tumbles regularly from the wall, we have to be better prepared for action than were the king's men, who found themselves so helpless in the fable. Whether it is as simple as a co-worker's getting upset over losing an important file or as complex and charged as a disaster that distorts or destroys the shape of people's lives, our sensitivity to our own role, and the resources of wisdom and action on which we can call, will make all the difference in whether we are genuinely helpful or not.

WHAT CAN WE DO?

By its very nature, a critical situation is usually brief, that is, limited by time in some way or other. The goal is ordinarily straightforward: to get the individual functioning again. This is different from trying to read hearts deeply or attempting to rebuild personalities. These objectives are common-sense ones; their achievement depends on our understanding of

1

them and of our own possibilities and limitations. Nothing replaces a level head and good human instincts: These are the elements in the foundation of our response in any difficult circumstances.

For those who are not full-time mental health workers, these qualities are absolutely essential. Combine them with some basic appreciation of the nature and course of emergencies and ordinary persons can—and, as a matter of fact, will—do very well in managing everyday crisis situations. If we understand what we can do, we are not only able to do it but we are also able to help others understand what they too can do in response to the circumstances. This knowledge in itself reduces the intensity of the problem and makes it more approachable. A sensible understanding of the steps to follow also liberates the strengths of all those associated with the problem, allowing them to employ their own skills in drawing available resources together from the environment.

Many nonprofessional counselors—clergy, lawyers, businessmen—discover that what they should do in emergency situations is what they already do instinctively anyway. That, however, is not true for all persons, some of whom relish the excitement of a crisis and tend to do things to prolong it rather than to bring it to an end. Others, possessing good hearts but little more, approach the problem more grandiosely, taking more responsibility than they should. In their stumbling attempts to be helpful, they often end up being just the opposite.

At times the person who is the central actor in the crisis may complicate the difficulty by not cooperating or by concealing resources, such as his or her family or friends. There is simply no substitute for individuals, even nonexperts, knowing their limitations and understanding the possibilities and boundaries of intervention. Then they are able to act in what at least passes for a professional manner. They can also define and assign roles to others in the manner of a good *triage* officer on a battlefield or in a hospital.

The main thing the knowledgeable professional can do when confronted with common crises is to reduce the impact of the crisis event and build a solid basis for the required steps of response. Crises are very disorganizing; a good response tends to put organization back into the emergency environment. One of the principal parameters of crisis situations is the pulsating sense of urgency that, as MacKinnon and Michels have observed, is analogous to pathological anxiety in other situations in that it cripples the person's capacity to respond and to use his or her own resources effectively. An economy of available energy exists in any emergency; like gasoline supplies it must be used wisely and to full effect. Idling or racing the motor not only adds noise and confusion but diminishes efficiency. The counselor of common sense sees clearly that a primary objective is to maintain self-control and not be overwhelmed by this infectious urgency. This is not just maintaining a stiff upper lip; it is an intelligent way to monitor the anxiety, for by reducing its effects upon oneself, one reduces its effect on the person at the core of the emergency. Nothing succeeds in an emergency like self-assurance, and one does not have to be an expert in order to possess it.

THE CRISIS-NEEDY

One must be wary of individuals who excessively enjoy crises and their atmosphere. They are, to some degree, like psychopaths who crack safes and rob museums because they crave the excitement that goes with such events and cannot take much pleasure in more ordinary events or relationships.

Living off crises is, for some, a substitute life, a distracting and totally absorbing commitment to the moods of danger and urgency that attend critical moments. When people need the crisis more than the crisis needs them, they reveal that they may get in the way instead of helping to clear it for others.

CRISIS STYLES

There are many ways in which crises may be analyzed. They may, for example, be seen as originating from within the psychic structure of the individual, as is clearly the case in certain psychological breakdowns. One may also observe a category of somatic crises, emergencies of the body system, such as strokes or heart attacks.

Another very large category in the classification of emergencies is the interpersonal realm, in which relationships such as those between married people or family members are the source and setting for the crisis reaction. Nonprofessionals are often the persons called first in such situations, either because those close at hand read the crisis as less serious than it is or because they do not, for one reason or another, wish to get involved in professional mental health treatment at that time.

It is also possible to conceptualize crises according to another framework. Edwin Shneidman, for example, discusses them in relationship to life-stages. Some occur during a stage of life and may be termed *intratemporal*. Here the crisis is specific to some period, such as adolescence or middle age. One can, in this schema, also place crises on an *intertemporal* continuum, that is, occurring at some juncture between life-stages. As Schneidman observes, "Many people can be adolescents quite successfully, but they have difficulty becoming adults." Many crises have their origins in the profoundly human difficulty of learning to surrender the previous stage of existence.

Beyond this, crises may also occur outside any time frame. We are frequently face to face with the mysterious when we examine this sort of emergency. Shneidman feels that such crises explain some of the otherwise "unaccountable suicides" that occur with bewildering regularity. What is the strand, hard as it is to detect, that may lead us back to an understanding of how these can occur? Such questions are important, although in this particular situation we may be called upon to deal with the individual's anxiety without any clear sense of what touched it off.

Such models of crisis development are obviously not mutually exclusive. Their value lies in the way they help us to sort out and think clearly about emergency problems. While such classifications do not solve problems, they may assist us in putting order into the unsettled atmosphere of the crisis event. It sometimes happens that the individual who wants to help possesses more willingness than good sense. Even professionals supposedly trained to maintain perspective sometimes intrude disastrously precisely because they haven't had a way of surveying the crisis with any objectivity. A system of classification enables us to penetrate and yet establishes some saving distance between ourselves and the incident in which we are called upon to intervene. The modern prejudice against classification and diagnosis is at times a symptom of a romantic view of our existence. Any construction that enables us to define and to perceive the crisis event more clearly is a valuable asset, especially for the nonprofessional in the field.

WHAT DO YOU DEAL WITH?

As nonprofessionals move into an emergency situation they ask, first of all, why this event, whatever its specific nature, should have occurred at this time in the person's life. This is another mode of attempting to answer *before* we do anything because, in large measure, its answer will tell us what to do.

Our concern in emergencies is with precipitating events, events with causes that brought out this reaction from the individual at this particular time. The objective of our intervention, as Schneidman notes, is to "undo the effects of the precipitants." The proper identification of the precipitant stress leads us to the event or circumstances that threw the individual out of balance and gave rise to the symptoms that he or she now experiences. This precipitant may bring psychological conflicts directly to the surface or it may affect the individual at a physiological level, with an evident symptom of physical impairment or illness. Whichever is the case, the person will reveal something of his or her basic self by reacting according to the patterns of character or personality structure.

Some people manage their anxiety better than others do, but however severe the obvious symptom, we need to trace it back to the stress that set it off. That becomes our immediate concern and the goal of our initial emergency response. We have to do something about the precipitating stress in order to intervene successfully. The emergency counselor, then, settles for short-term, immediate goals. As Howard Parad has put it, we are concerned with the "alleviation of the immediate impact of disruptive stressful events." Secondly, we want to help the person use his or her own resources to adapt to the stress. These include "the manifest and psychological capabilities and social resources of the directly affected . . . for coping with the effects of stress adaptively."

FUNDAMENTALS

The field of social work has long been deeply involved in crisis theory and technique. Much of the impetus for this involvement came from the work of Erich Lindemann, who worked with the survivors of the disastrous Coconut Grove fire in Boston in 1942. Gerald Caplan has also been a major influence and, along with Lindemann, has developed some basic principles about crises that should be reviewed by any nonprofessional who becomes involved in this field. Others who have since amended or expanded these notions include Lydia Rapaport, Howard Parad, David Kaplan, Gerald Jacobson, Marvin Strickler, and Peter Sifneos.

First of all, crisis situations are episodic in the life-span of individuals, families, groups, communities, and nations. Usually they are initiated by a hazardous event, which may be a blow from the outside or something that arises because of less bounded internal pressures. There may be one catastrophic event or a series of mishaps that have a cumulative effect.

Second, the basic human balance is disturbed and the individual is rendered vulnerable. He or she then goes through a customary series of responses in an attempt to regain balance. If these ordinary responses do not work, the anxiety grows and new methods must be used to restore the balance that has not been regained.

Third, if there is no resolution and the tension builds to a peak, then a *precipitating factor* can bring about the instant of crisis in which the balance is lost and the person suffers disorganization. This is the state of active crisis.

Fourth, the events that occur may be perceived by the individual under various rubrics: (1) as a threat to basic needs and independence; (2) as a loss of self-identity or some ability; or (3) as a challenge to survival, development, or mastery.

It follows that these perceptions will draw out of the person a characteristic emotional reaction. The meaning of this for the individual is reflected in different ways. If the event is perceived as a threat, anxiety will increase. If it is perceived as a loss, the individual will experience depression, deprivation, or mourning. If it is seen as a challenge, one may observe a moderate increase in anxiety but also the presence of incipient hope and expectation.

Fifth, the crisis situation is not essentially a sickness or a pathological experience. It is actually a realistic struggle, given the actual circumstances of the individual's life. This can touch off earlier conflicts that have been resolved or only partially resolved. The counselor will then observe inappropriate and exaggerated responses. The task of the crisis counselor may here be directed to (1) resolving the present difficulty; (2) reworking the previous struggle; and (3) dissolving the linkage between the two.

It must also be noted that each crisis has stages that can be predicted and mapped. These stages, therefore, can be anticipated, enabling the counselor to read the nature of a particular reaction in order to learn the point at which the person is blocked or stuck. Careful attention can help us understand why, for example, he or she cannot do what is termed their "crisis work" and master the situation.

Also, one can be fairly certain of the time limitation of the active crisis state. Between the first blow and the final resolution, the period of time may vary quite a bit, but the actual state of intense disequilibrium is limited by time. The outer limit is usually from four to six weeks.

During the resolution of the crisis, the affected person is generally ready to accept help. He or she is more available because his or her defenses may be down and previous patterns of coping may be disorganized. A little effort here can produce great improvement.

Last of all, during the stage in which the person reintegrates the self in order to enter once more into life, he or she may learn new and better ways of coping with future crisis situations. The inverse is also true, because if no help is available or given, the person may learn maladaptive solutions or patterns that will stand up poorly under future pressures.

For Further Reading

Alexander, Franz. "Psychoanalytic Contributions to Short-Term Psychotherapy." In *Short-Term Psychotherapy* (L. R. Wolberg, ed.). New York: Grune and Stratton, 1965.

Dublin, Louis I. *Suicide: A Sociological and Statistical Study*. New York: Ronald Press, 1963.

Erikson, Erik H. *Identity and the Life Cycle,* Mono. 1. New York: International Universities Press, 1959.

Farberow, Norman L., and Shneidman, Edwin L. *The Cry for Help*. New York: McGraw-Hill, 1961.

Fisher, Sheila. *Suicide and Crisis Intervention: Survey and Guide to Services*. New York: Springer, 1973.

Gill, Merton M. (ed.). *The Collected Papers of David Rapaport*. New York: Basic Books, 1967.

Hartmann, Heinz. *Ego Psychology and the Problem of Adaptation*. New York: International Universities Press, 1958.

Janis, Irving L. *Psychological Stress*. New York: John Wiley and Sons, 1958.

Kaplan, D. M., Smith, A., Grobstein, R., and Fischman, S. E. "Family Mediation of Stress." *Social Work* 18 (July 1973), pp. 60–69.

Kardiner, Abraham. *The Individual and His Society*. New York: Columbia University Press, 1939.

Klein, Donald C., and Lindemann, Erich. "Preventive Intervention in Individual and Family Crisis Situations." In *Prevention of Mental Disorders in Children* (G. Caplan, ed.). New York: Basic Books, 1961.

Lang, Judith. "Planned Short-Term Treatment in a Family Agency." *Social Casework* 55 (June 1974), pp. 369–74.

Lazarus, R. S., Averill, J. R., and Opton, E. M., Jr. "The Psychology of Coping: Issues of Research and Assessment." In *Coping and Adaptation* (G. V. Coelho, et al). New York: Basic Books, 1974.

Lindemann, Erich. "Symptomatology and Management of Acute Grief." *American Journal of Psychiatry* 10 (Sept. 1944).

McGee, Richard D. *Crisis Intervention in the Community*. Baltimore: University Park Press, 1974.

MacKinnon, Roger A., and Michels, Robert. *The Clinical Interview in Psychiatric Practice*. Philadelphia: W. B. Saunders & Co., 1972.

Morris, Betty. "Crisis Intervention in a Public Welfare Agency." *Social Casework* 49 (Dec. 1968), pp. 612–17.

Parad, Howard J., et al, (eds.). *Emergency and Disaster Management: A Mental Health Sourcebook*. Bowie, Md.: Charles Press, 1976.

Resnik, H. L. P., and Ruben, Harvey L. (eds.). *Emergency Psychiatric Care*. Bowie, Md.: Charles Press, 1975.

Selye, Hans. *The Stress of Life*. New York: McGraw-Hill, 1956.

Shneidman, E. S. "Crisis Intervention: Some Thoughts and Perspectives." In *Crisis Intervention*. (Spector, G. A. & Claiborn, W. C., eds.). New York: Behavioral Publications, 1973.

Shneidman, E. S., Farberow, N. L., and Litman, R. E. *The Psychology of Suicide*. New York: Science House, 1970.

White, Robert W. "Strategies of Adaptation: An Attempt at Systematic Description." In *Coping and Adaptation* (G. V. Coelho, D. A. Hamburg, and J. E. Adams, eds.). New York: Basic Books, 1974.

TWO

What Is a Crisis?

THE question seems simple enough, and everyone, even those with limited experience, has some kind of an answer. But our perception of a crisis situation may not match exactly the reality that operationally defines a truly critical incident or passage in a person's life. It is imperative that we examine ourselves carefully, especially if we are nonprofessional counselors, because whether we are conscious of it or not, we have already developed a style of crisis management. Teachers, clergy, funeral directors and other nonprofessional counselors are on the front lines every day and are constantly involved in assessing and processing emergency situations.

Indeed, emergencies may enter our lives on such a regular basis that we may fashion a way to deal with them in order to manage and minimize their potential effects on us. Our techniques, informal and unplanned as they may be, may in fact represent our manner of protecting ourselves from, and gathering strength for, the onslaught of personal problems that come regularly into our professional work. It is possible that what we have learned to do in adapting ourselves to our work may serve both our own interests and those of the persons with whom we work. It may also be, however, that we need to calibrate our responses more carefully so that we can insure that our responses are as truly helpful to others as they are to ourselves. Just as we readjust binoculars so that their enlarging function mediates best between ourselves and our environment, so we must focus freshly on emergencies in order to see them in authentic perspective. We must see them as entities separate from our own personalities, and we must understand at the same time the complex of personal needs or problems that may distort our perception and therefore strongly influence both the mode and the effectiveness of our response.

There are some counselors who involve their own personalities in their work to such an extent that their intervention changes the nature of the situation with which they are dealing. Some persons in every profession tend to exaggerate emergencies. They sniff them out and seem restless until they have discovered something wrong that needs immediate mending. They have what novelist Thomas Mann once described as a "sympathy for the abyss." Circling it constantly, they search for people swaying near its edge. They need crises the way free-fall parachutists need excitement; it is the fine edge of everyday life. Such people may do better to involve themselves in work that is specifically oriented toward emergency management, such as rescue teams and crisis hot lines.

In most professions, however, the emergency represents a break in the routine and therefore is a definable and distinct challenge when it arises. It is obviously essential for persons who may have to deal with emergencies, even on an irregular basis, to monitor their own interest in, and attitudes toward, the development of crises. Overenthusiasm may blur our perceptions and interfere with a sensible response to them. A need for crises or a habit of casting all situations in critical terms wears out the concept as well as the individuals involved.

It is equally obvious that a consistent underplaying of environmental occurrences can cause just as much if not greater distress. The fashion of remaining cool in whatever circumstances can introduce a distortion similar to that occasioned by overeagerness. Remaining calm in difficult moments is not the same as withdrawing defensively in order to shield oneself from the effects of involvement. Whether it is in a parish, a clinic, or a law office, one can readily discover individuals on either end of this continuum of inappropriate response. While the one who needs crises the way others need oxygen may resemble the boy who cried wolf, the excessively restrained counselor may interfere markedly, and with serious consequences, by refusing to identify and respond at the right time to a real crisis. Laid-back indifference in the style of the Rock of Ages is not ideal for crisis counseling. "Wait and see" works well in certain contexts, but it is not helpful in dealing with emergencies. By their nature, crises wait for no one.

HEALTHY OUTLOOK

Reasonably well-adjusted persons can easily identify the kinds of counselors just described. On their shoulders may fall the burden of managing not only the crisis but also these other colleagues so that their intervention is neither premature nor nonexistent. Nothing takes the place of the individual with basically healthy instincts who has both the proper information and, if possible, some training. The calm generated by these individuals is not that of the defensive individual but is rather the outcome of good sense and good ideas, properly integrated for the situation at hand. Nothing replaces common sense as the basic attribute of the individual who will offer the most helpful intervention in a crisis situation.

DIMENSIONS OF A CRISIS

It seems that we should be able to recognize a crisis just as easily as we would an earthquake or some other jarring event. The fact is, however, that there is no common definition that is used by professionals who are engaged day to day in dealing with crises. In a survey conducted in 1966 through questionnaires sent to 154 psychiatric emergency services, it was discovered that only twenty had any working definitions of emergencies or crises, and that no comprehensive definition was available at all (Glascotte, R. M., et al. *The Psychiatric Emergency*). Most of the respondents reported that they followed something akin to common sense and that they defined an emergency as a situation in which an individual had become dangerous to himself or to others, or, again, as a situation whose urgency was self-evident in that a person was clearly in need of supervision and protection.

In analyzing the results of this survey, J. K. Morrice (*Crisis Intervention*) lists a limited number of behaviors that emerge as obvious emergency situations: (1) attempted suicide (also called parasuicide); (2) assault; (3) destruction of property; (4) extreme anxiety amounting to panic; and (5) bizarre behavior evoking fear.

Nearly everyone, including the uninformed layperson, would identify these as crisis situations. In fact, unconsciously but wisely, they would add the element that is an essential note in our definition of these situations: They would say, "Somebody ought to do something about it." A crisis stands as an event that demands response; it is not for subtle observation or contemplation; it is not, like so many things in life, such as unanswered mail, something that will eventually take care of itself. It pressures its environment for response from outside that will relieve and resolve it. The nonprofessional counselor is often the person who must make the necessary response.

Crises can become our business whether we want them to or not. Some sense of their nature and some anticipation or rehearsal of our reactions can therefore be extremely helpful in preparing us to deal with what may be both unexpected and unpredictable. As has been mentioned, there are certain precipitating events that the respondent must be able to identify in order to be of assistance. It is also helpful to recognize the clusters of human situations in which such precipitants build up and finally coalesce into the dagger shape of an emergency. Studies in both Great Britain and the United States yield corresponding results in this regard.

FAMILY CONFLICTS

One of the leading sources from which emergencies can emerge full-blown is the family. Family conflicts include a wide range of behavior in addition to such obvious problems as marital discord and impending divorce. It may be helpful to note here that at times an entire family may experience a crisis together. Even when the crisis is focused sharply on an individual family member, there is frequently need to do something for the other family members, who are strongly affected although not directly involved in the emergency itself.

The usual precipitant is a social crisis, that is, something that flowers in the context of the relationships among family members. Under this heading may be listed many of the other common emergency problems: problems at work, problems with alcohol, financial difficulties, accidents, and a whole range of difficulties from illness to bereavement. If an individual displays significantly withdrawn behavior and does not seek assistance, then somebody else in the family should do it for him or her. The first contacts that nonprofessionals have concerning an emergency frequently come through those related or otherwise close to the affected person. The social environment is theoretically separable from the crisis, but in practical terms, it is not. Some awareness of those who are standing by and a readiness to respond to them are important aspects of what we are called upon to do.

Sometimes the family's limits are finally reached after a prolonged problem with one of its members. The capacity for tolerating behavior disturbing to the social unit suddenly comes to an end and a family member seeks outside help. This may be because of something the principally affected individual does or because of some shift in other circumstances. Whatever it is that throws the family's balance of adjustment off—an illness, a death, an unexpected financial strain—the result is the same in terms of the emergent crisis. Those who find that they are faced with doing something in such circumstances must be aware of the obvious complexity of any family system and of the intertwining of factors and personalities involved.

Not the least of the factors that the alert helper will keep in mind is the need to sort out the layers of relationship and involvement in the social matrix of the emergency itself. This requires a sensitive teasing out of the emotional filaments, and accomplishing this demands that the counselor maintain balance and objectivity. While the immediate emergency is given direct attention, these collateral relationships must also be appreciated and fully understood, both to help the individual and to provide assistance to the family itself.

"Family" may here be thought of in a metaphorical as well as in a real sense. It represents the community of relationships in which the critically affected individual is malfunctioning. This may be a college dormitory room, a submarine crew, or colleagues in group medical or legal practice. It may represent a special kind of life-style, such as that of a commune or religious order. Very similar considerations may have to be applied in all these situations.

SORTING IT OUT

There are always distinctive difficulties involved whenever we must respond to a person and his or her social context. This is true, for example, in marriage counseling, a process in which the helper hears two sides of a story. If it were possible to hear the accounts given by the in-laws, reality might rise up as complicated as it is in the Japanese movie *Rashomon,* in which many different views of one incident are recounted. The perspective of the one responding to the emergency may be distorted early in the situation if he or she is enlisted prematurely on the side of one of those involved. It is common to discover, for example, that central figures in the emergency may paint a blackened, distorted picture of close family members or friends as a result of their temporarily disturbed state. Those depicted as not helpful or as the source of the problem may turn out to be quite different when the situation is carefully evaluated.

A special problem arises if someone comes for help when he or she is already seeing someone else for psychological assistance. Anyone who has worked for even a short time in the helping professions will be familiar with the kinds of complaints that an individual may make about other professional people. Whether it is a complaint about a medical doctor, a psychologist, a teacher, or a lawyer, one should restrain any willingness to accept the charges at their face value. Indeed, even though the conditions of an emergency exist, one would generally interpret these as the complainant's distortions rather than as reliable representations of the actual situation.

Nonprofessionals can dangerously compromise themselves and their effectiveness by letting themselves be drawn off-side by these charges. Such negative statements should cause us to bear in mind the need to contact or establish some working relationship with previous therapists or supervisors. If there is time and it can be arranged, getting in touch with a person who has worked previously with—and may have technical responsibility for—the individual can be essential.

A rule of thumb for amateurs in the management of crises is to use the previous provider of assistance as the immediate source of information. The story that the individual tells may lead one to make incorrect judgments about the efficacy of previous treatment. This is a very complicated area, and for ethical and professional reasons one should suspend judgment on complaints about other professionals.

Generally these complaints represent what we understand as transference reactions, which have their origin in the individual's psychic structure. They may only reflect the fact that he or she has been actively engaged in a treatment that, because of unresolved conflicts, he or she is resisting. This will be discussed in greater detail later on, but even without further technical explanation, we recommend that nonprofessional helpers maintain enough distance from the emergency to judge it dispassionately and avoid choosing sides or making moral judgments in situations about which they are in fact, just beginning to learn.

SOME TYPES OF CRISIS

We may distinguish at this point three scenarios for the emergencies that may be presented to us.

In the first instance we find an individual for whom the crisis is not exactly new. That is to say, this person has been functioning for a long time under what might be described as emergency conditions. Some people bear up very well for lengthy periods in situations in which major ongoing stresses are present, such as the presence of an incapacitated spouse or elderly parents who need constant care. The crisis occurs when such a person reaches a point of exhaustion and can no longer cope adequately. This, for example, may be what happens to air-traffic controllers or other individuals in high-stress jobs.

Many people's lives are very much like these as far as their psychological circumstances are concerned; the traffic is heavy and unremitting. When a break in their ability to cope takes place, these persons clearly meet the criteria for crisis intervention. They are suffering a temporary, reversible reaction in which a definable precipitant can also be observed, even though the precipitant—just one too many days of pressure, for example—might not seem to be as major an incident in itself as those that touch off other situations. Such persons can recoup well with periods of rest and support.

Another type of crisis can arise when there is an unexpected change, such as the death of a loved one or the loss of a job or some other security, that triggers an overwhelming release of emotion. People involved in this kind of crisis find that they cannot deal with the ordinary demands of living and working; their ability to cope, but not their fundamental capacity, is crippled. This is one of the most common kinds of crises. Again, its temporary, reversible nature, as well as the immediate cause, can be identified.

A third kind of crisis is one in which the person may be the active rather than the passive agent. Some people design and originate their own crises. These crises possess what has been termed a "purposive element" and are not emergencies in the same sense as the ones described above.

THE RIGHT ANGLE

The person confronted with a crisis needs to evaluate the situation from two positions: one that is close-up and enables a clear view of exactly what condition the individual is in, and the other from a middle distance, where there is the saving perspective that provides a broader and deeper view of the individual in context and in relationship to his or her motivations and needs. Why has this crisis happened at this point? Why has it happened to this individual? These are not the aggressive or hostile inquiries that newspeople often make at the time of emergencies. They are rather the calm and measured questions that persons who sincerely want to understand must ask, at least of themselves, to guarantee that they have properly identified a crisis and grasped its rudimentary characteristics before they make any additional moves.

For Further Reading

Argles, P., and Mackenzie, M. "Crisis Intervention with a Multiproblem Family: a Case Study." *Journal of Child Psychology and Psychiatry* 11 (1970), pp. 187–95.

Bloom, B. L. "Definitional Aspects of the Crisis Concept." *Journal of Consulting Psychology* 27 (1963), pp. 498–502.

Butcher, J. N., and Maudal, G. R. "Crisis Intervention." In *Clinical Methods in Psychology* (I. B. Weiner, ed.). New York: John Wiley and Sons, 1976.

Decker, J. B., and Stubblebine, J. M. "Crisis Intervention and Prevention of Psychiatric Disability: a Follow-up Study." *American Journal of Psychiatry* 129 (1972), pp. 725–29.

Duckworth, G. L. "A Project in Crisis Intervention." *Social Casework* 48 (1967), pp. 227–31.

Eastham, K., Coates, D., and Allodi, F. "The Concept of Crisis." *Canadian Psychiatric Association Journal* 15 (1970), pp. 463–71.

Glascotte, R. M., et al. *The Psychiatric Emergency.* Washington, DC: The Joint Information Service of APA and NAMH, 1966.

Halpern, H. "Crisis Theory: a Definitional Study." *Community Mental Health Journal* 9 (1973), pp. 342–49.

Hoffman, D. L., and Remmel, M. L. "Uncovering the Precipitant in Crisis Intervention." *Social Casework* 56 (1975), pp. 259–67.

Jacobson, G. F. "Crisis Theory and Treatment Strategy: Some Sociocultural and Psychodynamic Considerations." *Journal of Nervous and Mental Diseases* 141 (1965), pp. 209–18.

Kaplan, D. M. "Observations on Crisis Theory and Practice." *Social Casework* 49 (1968), pp. 151–55.

Langsley, D. G., and Kaplan, D. *The Treatment of Families in Crisis.* New York: Grune and Stratton, 1968.

Meltzoff, J., and Kornreich, M. *Research in Psychotherapy.* New York: Atherton, 1970.

Morrice, J. W. *Crisis Intervention.* New York: The Pergamon Press, 1976.

Parad, H. J. (ed.). *Crisis Intervention: Selected Readings.* New York: FSAA, 1965.

Specter, G. A., and Claiborn, W. L. *Crisis Intervention.* New York: Behavioral Publications, 1973.

Wolkon, G. H. "Crisis Theory, the Application for Treatment, and Dependency." *Comprehensive Psychiatry* 13 (1972), pp. 459–64.

THREE

Common Sense

COMMON sense remains a rare and extremely valuable commodity. In emergency situations there is no substitute for it. Nonprofessional counselors can, in fact, travel a long way merely on the strength derived from this resource. Common sense, for example, generates a certain modesty of therapeutic claim and ambition; it inspires and steadies us in our activity, so that we do not try to be anything but ourselves in our work with others. It also reassures us that, with limited objectives and a clear sense of our identity, we can function quite adequately in crisis situations.

What does common sense tell us about ourselves and what we can do when we are challenged by emergencies?

First of all, it informs us that we need not perceive ourselves as long-term therapists. We are not out to identify and resolve all the conflicts that may be present in the persons who experience crisis situations in their lives. Our attempt to be helpful should have a clear focus, so that we do not extend our responsibility or our intervention beyond the boundaries of the emergency itself.

Secondly, even though we offer many references to works in the field throughout these pages, we do not feel that we are necessarily called or obliged to transform ourselves into crisis specialists after the model of those professionals who devote themselves to this field. We retain our primary identity as educators, lawyers, or members of the clergy who have refined our sensitivity and capacity to respond to what may be considered *atypical* experiences. These experiences, even though they may occur regularly, do not represent the kinds of activities we engage in on a day-to-day basis. The teacher teaches, the lawyer writes briefs, and the clergy member engages in the gamut of ordinary pastoral experi-

17

ences. Their daily lives are all at times punctuated with emergencies, and it is to these crises, in fairly precise and limited fashion, that we give our energies, harnessed and shaped by information and good judgment.

THE CHIEF WORK

Similarities exist across all professions that offer service to other persons. The common denominator is an effort to understand others in the context of their lives. This involves us—even in pressured, emergency situations—in a steady effort to recognize and read accurately the signs and symbols (words, gestures, unconscious communication) through which others reveal themselves in three-dimensional psychological aspects. Understanding is a familiar concept, and most nonprofessional counselors appreciate that it requires a listening attitude, a readiness to suspend judgment, and a capacity for placing themselves in the position of others. It does not demand that we agree or disagree; understanding requires a willingness to inspect the life-space of other individuals and to see, at least briefly, the world through their eyes.

Such notions merely define the quality of understanding that we can recognize in our own lives; we know it when we experience it, and we have some sense of its unique power to support and move us forward even when we are faced with severe obstacles. It generates a quality of "being with" others that, if it does not take their burdens away, makes it possible for them to carry those burdens more bravely and with greater confidence in their own powers. Such understanding remains a vital and indispensable quality for all nonprofessionals who find themselves engaged in counseling work, even if only at times of emergency.

Understanding also suggests that we have learned to interpret the significance of subtle communications from others. This does not mean that we impose meaning from only our own viewpoint, as we do, for example, when we finish sentences for others—only to discover that they were actually about to say something else. Understanding does not leap to conclusions that others are not ready to make for themselves. This occurs when we are caught up in what could be called the screenwriter's syndrome: a readiness to invent or otherwise supply the details of other people's lives from our own imaginations. Sensing unconscious or symbolic communications, even when they are half-formed, is a more demanding service to perform. It cannot occur unless we empty ourselves of our own wildest hunches and distractions so that we can accurately receive the messages that others are sending.

OBJECT OF UNDERSTANDING

Having factored out the interference that springs from our own mus-ings, we are in a better position to catch the essential communications of others, even when these are transmitted in heavily symbolic fashion. This is a necessary dimension for understanding, particularly in crisis situations, because the compressed time frame makes our task of accu-rate understanding more urgent. Sharpening our capacity to receive and to read confused and blurred human communication will make us far more confident and effective in crisis situations.

For example, in periods of mourning there may be significant amounts of symbolic communication that tell us that the individual is caught up in performing what Freud termed "grief work." To misunderstand, for instance, the symbolic search for the lost person, which has been iden-tified as an aspect of this grief work, and see it, from the outside, as aimless or irrational activity on the part of the bereaved could lead us, even with the best of intentions, to interventions that might prove to be interferences in a necessary human process. Learning when to stand by and let people mourn leads to the kind of response that such symbolic communication deserves. When we can stand with people in the crisis of mourning, or help others to do it without becoming too excited at some of its manifestations, then we are in a very real sense speaking with deep understanding to the grieving person. Deep, in this situation, truly calls to the deep.

The same may be said about other instances of "acting out" that may occur in families, when, for example, one of the children begins to fail subjects at school or to behave in ways previously uncharacteristic of him or her. The effort to understand the symbolic significance of these events instead of trying, for example, to correct them through punish-ment leads to a far more sensible and therapeutic intervention.

REACTING SENSIBLY

Nonprofessional counselors are not expected to be perfect in their response to psychological emergencies; nobody, not even mental health professionals, can be effective if they hold up an impossible ideal for themselves. The teacher or the undertaker, along with other nonpsychological professionals, acknowledges limitations and necessar-ily responds within certain restrictions. Reacting sensibly may mean settling in almost every situation for something less than the ideal solution to the critical problem. We are not, however, looking for perfect so much as human resolutions of emergency situations. Scaling down our expectations so that we do not feel guilty if we fall short of meeting them means that our genuine strengths will be more available for use in the critical moments.

We may be able only to relieve the symptoms of the person afflicted by some adversity. Complete cures are not possible within the confines of our customary engagement with an emergency. The time available to us can, however, be used quite well even if we achieve only what appear to be low-level goals. In an emergency it is a distinct accomplishment to help other persons to keep going or to start going again. Helping people make it through the night is not a task to be disdained by any of us.

Coupled with this may be judgments that at least restrain us or others involved in the emergency from doing something that would be directly harmful. These factors are usually clear in physical emergencies, in which most people know that it is not sensible to move an injured person before medical aid has arrived. Psychological parallels also exist, so that we do not, at a vulnerable time of emotional crisis, press too strongly on the instinctive defenses of the affected individual. Confronting persons to make them confess that they made a mistake or to admit the truth about some past event is the psychological counterpart of giving the wrong medical treatment to a person suffering a stroke.

Proper preparation and knowledge of how to make a referral for continued management of the crisis—including for possible extended therapeutic care—are essential for any nonprofessional who may, even on only an occasional basis, have to deal with crisis situations. Discovering local resources for psychological and social interventions and having a list of those available border on being an ethical requirement for such nonprofessionals. It may also be useful to establish some relationship with helpers in the community so that easy and effective referrals can be made at times of crisis.

Nonprofessional helpers also face critical situations in which they at times find that they are the only available resource. It is with this particular challenge that we are especially concerned here: There are frequently specific "tasks," as David Kaplan has described them, for each crisis situation. Some grasp of these will provide the nonprofessional with points of reference as well as with a secure foundation for his or her common-sense response in difficult situations. Before we deal with these suggestions, a few issues that have plagued nonprofessional helpers remain to be discussed.

THERAPEUTIC CLICHÉS

America has democratized psychological treatment. Over the past several years there has been a systematic downgrading of the role of professionals in assisting the emotionally disturbed. While one of the benefits of this trend has been the invigoration of community resources and the encouragement of nonprofessionals to develop their counseling skills, it has also given birth to hackneyed and naïve models of how to help people with their emotional problems. Some people actually try to offer treatment through the modality of the therapeutic cliché. What does this mean and why does the nonprofessional need to examine it carefully?

The explosion of psychological training in America has turned out large numbers of persons who know a little bit—at times a very valuable little bit—about counseling. Often the knowledge such persons possess is fragmentary, and they feel their inadequacies keenly. While they wish to develop their skills, they are often unable to do this through systematic education. They end up doing what they can with whatever information and training they have been able to acquire.

Sadly enough, just such people, awash in both good will and good intentions, become the victims of oversimplified psychological notions and prefabricated counseling structures. These tend to obscure their own natural human strengths and make them and all other nonprofessionals sound alike. They want to do the right thing, but they are so determined to do this that their own healthy individuality—along with their capacity to respond directly to people—is blurred through their use of the formulalike responses that are the therapeutic clichés of our age. Such structures, or self-conscious models of the way a person should behave and speak as a counselor, interfere with one's basic capacity to help others.

STOCK RESPONSES

Such persons may be identified—or may identify themselves—through the phrases that they repeatedly use. Perhaps the most prominent of these clichés is "I think I hear you saying . . ." This precedes every response and is a prime symptom of the individual who counsels by the letter rather than by the spirit. People who frame everything with such introductory remarks or use the same response over and over again within the context of a helping situation—"I think you're feeling a lot of anger about this" is another example—reduce their own personal presence to a species of echo. They attempt to sound like some mythical counseling master and end up not sounding like themselves at all. "Would you like to share about this?" is the kind of question that overuses an important word and diminishes human communication at the same time. People who are in a close relationship never ask each other whether they want to share or not. They simply do it, without watching themselves do it. The introduction of stock phrases, in other words, tends to increase the self-consciousness of helpers and thereby decreases their effectiveness.

Yet another sign of this is the determined effort on the part of some helpers to apply a model of counseling whether it fits or not. Working with the dying, for example, has become almost a fad, and the awkward effort to make every terminally ill person pass through the stages of dying proposed by Kubler-Ross is an example of the psychological cliché at its worst. Because many models have been developed for crisis situations a special danger exists that helpers may attempt to impose them, whether they are steps, phases, or tasks, as though they were literal, rigid, and unalterable modes of procedure. We have to let people die in their own way, and suffer crises in their own way, if we are truly to help them.

MORE THAN FORMULAS

Emergencies are not occasions that are helped by people who are hobbled by psychological clichés. The penalty falls on them as well as on the person affected by the crisis. Helpers need to be liberated from this web of pseudocounseling for their own sake as well as for the sake of those they want to help. This is a situation in which a little learning is definitely a dangerous thing because it inhibits the healthy instincts of helpers, forcing them into a contorted mode of modified client-centered therapy that, in psychology's favorite word, is "inappropriate" for the situation.

Freeing people from the snarls of these ready-cut statements is essential because their excessive use blinds helpers to what is actually happening in those they attempt to assist. They respond to everyone in the same way and then wonder why they are not getting anywhere. Helping others, especially in crises, is difficult enough by itself, and it can be seriously compromised by persons who put more faith in a formulation than in their own good instincts. Many helpers experience chronic guilt about their therapeutic shortcomings without any awareness that it is not so much their fault as it is that of the overpopularized and oversimplified formulas of response in which they are overinvested.

In crises, time has a special significance. Helpers should try to hone their skills so that their understanding of the persons involved will be facilitated rather than complicated and delayed by such cliché-ridden structures. Getting to the heart of the matter is vital, and we are far more successful when we move humanly and sensibly, unburdened by the weight of such interferences.

SOMETHING THAT WORKS

The directly human response always works best. This is an abiding truth that should be a source of encouragement and strength for non-professionals who are involved in crisis situations. Just as no legal brief, however complicated, can replace the simple declarative sentence of human intentions, so no technique, no matter how sophisticated, can replace the human foundation on which it must ultimately rest.

There is a special value to the plainly human response in crisis situations. Common sense coincides here with the technical analysis, which recognizes the value of our maintaining our status as separate individuals with clear identities of our own. When we are distinct individuals we minimize the distortion of our presence and our intentions by the person at the center of the crisis. He or she cannot read into our motives or our purposes when we make them clear right from the start. There is, however, a strong tendency to distort others when they are shadowy or vague figures; the affected person can more easily project onto them his or her own fears and conflicts. We need freedom of movement in crises, and we can maintain this best if we are, quite simply, ourselves rather than a mysterious "expert" or master therapist.

BEING YOURSELF

What does it mean for us to be ourselves? It does not suggest that we burden the person we are trying to help with our life stories or that we unnecessarily intrude in the situation. Nor does it mean, as some naïve therapists think, that we should tell them our own troubles. Being ourselves requires nothing quite so aggressive or, at times, self-serving. There is a simplicity and lack of self-consciousness about being ourselves that we either understand immediately or never will; we cannot pretend it. Most healthy people know this, and what they need is to be freed from the intimidation of the therapeutic cliché. They don't have to withhold themselves or their opinions as though the utterance of any of these things might dissolve some mystique.

Relying on ourselves relieves us of burdens that we might otherwise feel that we had to assume. We don't all have to sound like Freud, Carl Rogers, or some character out of a book or a movie. There is only specious magic in blurring our own personalities. We practically invite distortion on the part of the person under the pressure of crisis when we do this, and that can only impede us in our efforts to help.

This also allows us to stay away from territory in which we really don't know the way. We want to concentrate on just this exposed area of crisis, not on everything that went before and certainly not on everything that may follow. The best analogy may be the surgical field, in which a carefully delimited area is laid bare and dealt with.

Concentrating on the emergency, in the terms in which we have defined it, allows us to do what we can at the moment. It also makes it possible for us to refer the individual elsewhere for further help in a much clearer manner. Referral is almost always one of our goals, and by being ourselves and confining ourselves to what we can comfortably do, we can move toward this with relative ease. By remaining ourselves and keeping some distance from the potential entanglements of overambitious involvement in the situation, we can step aside and let someone else take over without causing unnecessary trauma in the process. When we have been perceived unambiguously and with minimum distortion and when we exercise discipline in our response to the situation, we remain free enough to be truly helpful.

For Further Reading

Golan, N. "When Is a Client in Crisis?" *Social Casework* 50 (1969), pp. 389–94.

Golan, N. *Treatment in Crisis Situations*. New York: The Free Press, 1978.

Holmes, T. H., and Rohe, R. H. "The Social Readjustment Rating Scale." *Journal of Psychosomatic Research* 11 (1967), pp. 213–18.

Jacobson, G. F. "Programs and Techniques of Crisis Intervention." In *American Handbook of Psychiatry,* 2nd ed. (S. Arieti, ed.) New York: Basic Books, 1974.

Kennedy, E. *On Becoming a Counselor*. New York: Seabury Press, 1976.

Specter, G. A., and Claiborn, W. C. (eds.) *Crisis Intervention*. New York: Behavioral Publications, 1973. See especially: I. N. Korner, "Crisis Reduction and the Psychological Consultant"; N. Sebolt, "Crisis Intervention and Its Demands on the Crisis Therapist"; J. E. Williams, "Crisis Intervention Among the Bereaved: A Mental Health Consultation Program for Clergy."

FOUR

Approaching the Crisis

WHEN we are called in at the time of a crisis we do well to remember that we are hardly ever dealing with just the individual at the center of the unfolding story. Almost always the crisis represents a break in a system that is complex, intertwined, and derives its energy from varied sources. The person in direct focus is in a delicate relationship with family, friends, and business or work associates. All of these may somehow be interrelated, and they cannot be ignored if we are trying to understand what has really happened.

Information about the emergency will come directly or indirectly from all of those who are members of our system of relationships and from all those involved with the person or persons who are in the critical spotlight. It is not too much to say that a certain outline or image of the problem can be discerned from the reactions of all those who, metaphorically at least, stand around the central characters in the emergency drama. Entering a crisis situation, then, we should be ready to pick up as many cues as we can. They all are part of what is occurring, and if we wish to read the situation accurately, we will need to take into account all the bits and pieces of information, direct and indirect, available to us.

DON'T BE LOGICAL

We do not want to overemphasize the rational aspect of the crisis even though we attempt to impose a framework of reason on it. Its roots, as those of so much human behavior, are often tangled in the shifting earth of irrational and unconscious behavior. People's lives, the lives of their families and even their jobs may be distended by the emotional pressures of the crisis situation. While it is commonplace for us to attempt to force these misshapen structures back into reasonable containment, we discover the truth only when we make room for nonrational motivations that can so strongly affect those who are involved. Being prepared for irrationality in a larger picture, making at least tentative connections between things that seem remotely related, and understanding that there will be an impression, much like that of a signet ring in wax, on all those close to the affected persons, enables us to make reliable judgments both about the time dimension of the emergency and the way to deal with it.

How Are We Perceived?

We have previously discussed the helper's sense of identity in crisis situations. Others often see us very differently from the way we see ourselves. In emergency problems, people tend to invest us, even if we are not psychological experts, with authority that we feel we do not deserve. It is not our role to apologize or to disown this authority. It would be difficult to alter their expectations even if we tried to because these flow from their own needs; we can, however, get a sense of their dependent needs at the moment of crisis.

Being granted the role of the "expert" can be disadvantageous in certain circumstances but is extraordinarily helpful in an emergency. Having the authority enables us to act—to do something—rather than just reflect or plan about it. We are not beginning what may turn into extensive therapy; we are trying to sort out a confused situation and to get the process of life moving again for those affected by some adverse condition. Realizing that our role is not one of advocacy for one or the other of those people who are members of the system involved in the emergency is also helpful. We are consultants, as many crisis experts have noted, to a *situation* rather than to an individual. This distinction enables us to preserve the neutral perspective that is essential for seeing the full dimensions of the problem and for keeping it from getting worse while we are trying to make it better.

Transference and Countertransference

Transference feelings are those feelings currently being expressed that really have their origin in a person's past experience. Such feelings are unconscious and reveal the individual's shape as an infant and his or her other early experiences. When counselors intervene in someone else's life they can expect to be the object of transference as feelings, developed earlier toward others, are now displaced onto them. Transference reactions occur regularly in life, especially to people who are in positions of authority; they are often on the receiving end of feelings that are really appropriate to the leading characters in the subject's childhood. Full-time psychotherapists understand that a correct appreciation for and management of the transference feelings is essential for proper diagnosis and planning of treatment. The same is true of countertransference reactions, which are the feelings that come out of the therapist's own past experience that are displaced onto the client. While we refer only briefly to these traditional notions and do not expect nonprofessional counselors to become experts in the field, neither do we believe that they can be naïve about the existence or meaning of these subtle but pervasive phenomena.

The most important thing for helpers to understand about transference is that these feelings are not really directed toward them personally. These are emotions that are projected, like a movie onto a screen, and while they seem to be directed toward a counselor, they are really the reenactment of past relationships with other persons. When we observe them we actually get a cross-section of the basic dynamic structure of the person we are trying to help. Transference reactions are characteristically marked by feelings of ambivalence, and the therapist, like a lightning rod, draws them positively or negatively, even though they are intended for others.

Managing transference therapeutically is the business of experts, but everybody can at least understand that the rage or the overwhelming dependency that one may encounter in another individual is not to be taken personally. Such feelings, if held at a distance although not treated coldly or harshly, can tell us a great deal about those we are trying to help.

DON'T BE AN EXPERT

Practically speaking, nonprofessionals should not try to interpret these feelings or try to get to the bottom of them through some technique of confrontation; neither should they think that resolving them is the immediate task of intervention in a crisis situation. In an emergency, no therapist should treat transference feelings as though they were the main "stuff" of the therapeutic response. We do not want to open up what may be bound together by the transference feelings, distorted and irrelevant as they may seem in the situation. These are functional defenses and are not to be tampered with. Indeed, we may wish to use them to serve as a bridge toward the next step, which may well be referral. If a person transfers the feelings of dependence toward us, for example, we may allow that to go on even though we recognize that this dependent yielding toward us is not personal and that it comes out of a previous aspect of the person's life history. It creates, if used properly, a source of support during the time of the emergency, and we should allow the dependency to continue unexplored while we try to get through the most difficult part of the experience.

EMOTIONAL INVOLVEMENT

"Emotional involvement" is the painful price paid by people who have no understanding of the meaning of transference reactions. They become involved with feelings that have no direct reference to them, and then they cannot understand what is happening to them. They are frequently hurt, precisely because their good intentions are not a substitute for real knowledge.

The reason for the establishment of professional approaches in medicine, psychology, and other helping professions is to guarantee some distance—though not the cold and barren distance of rejection—in and through which a truly helpful relationship is to the other can be developed. Such neutral ground is essential; it is the only place where we can confidently stand. Getting overinvolved emotionally at the time of an emergency makes counselors unhelpful and at times destructive. They may become a part of the problem and find it very difficult to provide any kind of solution for others or for the cruel entanglements in which they find themselves snared.

MORE ON TRANSFERENCE

Because the response that nonprofessionals are asked to give in a crisis situation is extremely limited in its scope, the transference feelings of the client are not interpreted even when we may be fully aware of their presence. What we want to achieve is a positive relationship marked with good feelings on the conscious level. There is no effort to disturb or mobilize the feelings that are below the surface; we do not try to ferret out hidden meanings even though we may be picking up clear messages from the unconscious of the affected individual. Our understanding of the transference phenomenon can be used in the same way we would refer to a chart showing the varying depths of a body of water: We want a safe passage across the depths without trying to plumb them for all the information they contain.

As Paul Dewald has pointed out ("The Therapeutic Process: Resistance, Regression and Conflict," in *Psychotherapy, A Dynamic Approach*), our objective in supportive therapies is to strengthen the individual's defenses and to avoid doing anything that might unnecessarily intensify unconscious conflicts that cannot be dealt with in a brief time. We want, in other words, to avoid moves that would cause the person to regress psychologically. Individuals have enough trouble when they are in a crisis, and we want to help hold them together rather than reconstruct their personalities.

In order to strengthen their defenses, for example, we may consciously do things that are based on an understanding of their unconscious transference feelings even though we do not want to bring these into the light. How do we do that? Their defenses are the superstructure that rises from and yet at the same time transforms their true inner conflicts; defenses are what enable people to go on living without dealing with the unconscious reality of their lives. So, for example, we may feel their strong dependency needs even though they do not acknowledge them to themselves. They may defensively describe themselves as self-confident and independent while, at the unconscious level, they clearly project a need to lean on someone else.

As we move into the emergency situation we may feel them leaning on us. As mentioned before, we not only let them do this but we may also want to strengthen their defenses by assuming a fairly authoritarian stance in our dealings with them. This is the kind of thing that, for example, a great military leader often does in relation to his troops. Thus Caesar wore a red cloak onto the battlefield, and generals such as George S. Patton employed elaborate histrionic effects in order to magnify their role as leader and thus intensify their troops' trust in and willingness to follow their orders. So it is in a crisis. We may do much better by playing the role of the authority instead of rejecting it (as happens in much contemporary counseling theory and technique) because of the strong positive effect authority may have on the situation.

What we do in an emergency is to gratify some of an individual's needs on a conscious level in order to prevent any eruption from areas deeper down inside. This is one way of maintaining persons through difficult moments. So we may willingly assume and capitalize on the parental role because we can more effectively provide the reassurance and direction that are necessary to assist the person through the crisis: We can set limits, thereby supplying a measure of control at a moment of disorder, and we can reassure them about distressing thoughts and fantasies that may arise in the emotional upheaval of the emergency.

NEGATIVE AND POSITIVE . . .

On the other hand, we can also use our awareness of the possibility of negative transference to guide us so that we do not misinterpret hostile or angry outbursts on the part of the individuals with whom we are working. Instead of getting involved with interpreting such feelings as resistance, we can simply permit the persons to vent these strong reactions, allowing them to focus on something either in our relationship with them or in their relationship with, for example, a family member or a friend. Even though these expressions of anger are inappropriate, we allow them to stand without challenge.

By emphasizing the positive rapport without getting into the unconscious feelings we create a situation in which those being helped will be more ready to respond favorably in the future should another crisis arise. Their conscious attitude toward those who have helped them will be positive. As a final observation, we suggest that it may be wise to try to direct their transference feelings toward the institution we represent— toward the clinic, the parsonage, or the crisis hot line—rather than toward an individual helper who may or may not be on duty when a future crisis arises. This is, in fact, the kind of thing that happens anyway. We have all heard people say things like "I know whenever I feel bad I can go to the clinic and somebody will help me."

GETTING INFORMATION

One of the ways in which counselors called into an emergency can both stabilize the crisis and add markedly to their capacity to be helpful is through an orderly gathering of important information; nobody should fly blind into an emergency no matter how severe it may seem or how urgently it needs a response. There are basic facts that must be collected. This information is extremely important both for seeing the situation in perspective and for drawing up an acceptable plan of action. These facts include the names and addresses of the persons principally affected by the situation, as well as the names and addresses of all those others who may be part of the psychological system, whether it be a family, an office, or a school, that has been disrupted by the crisis. One should also try to ascertain the relationships, whether blood or friendship, of those who are part of the emergency event. It is common sense to also get the phone numbers of relatives, friends, and even the individual's family doctor.

WHAT'S MISSING?

In gathering information of this nature at a crisis time, nonprofessionals should be aware that the people involved may omit a great deal. This is to be expected of those who are suffering from the impact of a severe problem and whose emotional state may interfere markedly with their capacity to recall all the details of the events that have befallen them. These gaps or amnesia-like episodes are in themselves significant. They are almost always connected with important dimensions of the person's life, and as we can fill them in, we gain significant information about the inner world and perceptions of the persons who are feeling the crunch of the emergency.

Much of this can be accomplished through the traditional process of history-taking. While nonprofessionals may not be familiar with this, it is standard procedure in hospitals, clinics, and other places in which people seek medical or psychological assistance. Of itself, the taking of a person's life history, including the relevant material just discussed, puts some order into a fragmented and troubling time in life. History-taking is not designed merely to make the counselor seem like he or she knows what to do. It is a sensible procedure that restores perspective and helps the individual to begin to put his or her own experiences back into context. There is no magic in history-taking, but it has a calming effect on the individual. It also gives us a chance to observe the other person for indications of transference feelings or other phenomena that may prove important.

WHAT IS IMPORTANT?

As a part of the history-taking, the helper should find out about the individual's work, place of residence, religion, and even something about his or her relative place in society. It is possible that a crisis has different meanings at different socioeconomic levels. To this end, one must always pursue the question, "What is the meaning of this event in the life of the person suffering the crisis?" This is a second cousin to asking ourselves, "Why did this happen now?", a question designed to help us to identify the factor that precipitated the crisis.

History-taking should be under the control of the helper. If it is not structured, the individual may well use it, quite unconsciously, to act out and to express emotions that cannot be contained successfully by an information-seeking interview. The interview is meant, in other words, not only to gain important facts but to impose a certain structure that in itself creates a kind of balance in the person's reactions. We do not assist others when we merely let them break down during the history-taking or when we let them take over the questioning by expanding too much on one aspect of their story. While we note these behaviors for their psychological significance—as evidence about the important issues in their lives—we do not want to let them get out of hand. All these things can be discussed at length later on. Those intervening in a crisis must always remind themselves that they are not "treating" the person, nor are they engaged in resolving conflicts of lifelong duration. They are trying to help people cope and restore themselves to activity after a battering and disorganizing life event. The role of an interviewer is not helped, nor is the situation, if we let the interview slip out of control.

CONFIDENTIALITY TRAP

One of the things that may open up, especially for those who have not had much experience with emotional problems, is what we might term the "confidentiality trap." The subject or subjects involved in the crisis attempt to compromise helpers by getting them to promise confidentiality about the information that is given. This effort, which is frequently a characteristic part of the client's style and is therefore an aspect of transference, must be perceived in the overall context of his or her life. These attempts to bind us with confidentiality really tell us more about the person we are dealing with, and while we do not wish to become cynical, neither do we wish to approach such situations naïvely.

If we accept the imposition of confidentiality, we may lose our capacity to be of any assistance. How does this tactic work? One member of a family may admit to heavy drinking, something that contributed to the crisis, but may ask the helper not to divulge this to anybody else in the family. In truth, everybody in the family probably already knows about it. Such is the nature of what we call "family secrets." We must not too readily accept any such limitation of our freedom.

Our main objective is to steer clear of having our freedom to speak or to act curtailed by an early involvement in a promise that will be very difficult for us to keep. Rosenbaum and Beebe (*Psychiatric Treatment Crisis/Clinic/Consultation*) use the term *pseudoconfidentiality* to describe this situation. Those who are trying to help in an emergency cannot afford to be caught up in such a web of maneuvers; these efforts at manipulation can actually help us to understand how the person got into the crisis. We should therefore make clear that we are not promising anything about what we can or cannot say to others. It is a simple thing to say, "I understand your need for confidentiality, but I cannot promise that I will keep all this material secret. It may be important that I divulge some of it in order to help you." However we convey our meaning, it is vital that we do so and not allow ourselves to be bound in an area in which we need freedom.

THE EVENT ITSELF

In the history-taking we want to be sure that we get the event itself into proper perspective. When we enter the emergency we may have only a general idea of what really took place. We cannot act on such presumptions, nor should we assume that we can fill in the blank spaces by hunches or other such intuitive reactions. Exploring precisely what took place, in its exact setting and sequence, does not turn us into detective or annoying interrogators. Rather, it makes us sensitive and cautious helpers who know that this information must be obtained carefully if we are to be of assistance in resolving the emergency problem.

We may wish to inquire about whether such crises have occurred previously in the individual's life. Very often the affected person is no stranger to whatever has happened, whether it be family strife, an alcoholic binge, or getting fired from a job. If it has happened before, it may be very helpful to find out how it happened then and what resources were used in helping the person get through that crisis. It may be possible to use the same combination successfully once again. In connection with this, it is helpful to find out what parties were involved in the previous event and whether and where we can contact them. The names and addresses of professional helpers who may have become involved at the time are also important. They may prove to be the best sources of referral during this emergency as well.

We must also ask ourselves steadily that question about why the crisis has appeared at this time. Very often the person can tell you this directly: "My wife left me" or "I got fired from my job." Such clear statements provide us with the core of the critical problem. We can proceed on the old principle that people are always trying to tell us the truth. Sometimes they do this in indirect and twisted ways, but if we give them a chance, they will try to put together for us as complete and true a picture as possible of what happened to them and why—even in an emergency. The

truth comes to us in many ways, and we miss it only if we close ourselves off unnecessarily to its sources in an emergency situation.

For Further Reading

Dewald, Paul A. *Psychotherapy: A Dynamic Approach.* 2nd ed. New York:
Basic Books, 1971.

Rosenbaum, C. P., and Beebe, J. G., III. (eds.) *Psychiatric Treatment Crisis/
Clinic/Consultation.* New York: McGraw-Hill, 1975.

FIVE

Depression

EVERY counselor needs some familiarity with and sensitivity to the phenomenon of depression. In one way or another it enters into everyone's life. The recognizable mood of being down, however, is far different from the experience of severe depression that is often an indication that an individual is slipping into or is dealing with a major personal crisis. Depression of this sort is widely found even though it is not always recognized for what it is. One of the reasons for the difficulties we have in dealing with depression is that it is not a cut-and-dried phenomenon, and there are, even within the scientific ranks of the most reliable psychologists and psychiatrists, sharp divisions of opinion concerning its diagnosis and treatment.

DISTINCTIONS

Even nonprofessionals need some familiarity with the current scientific understanding of depression and the various ways in which it manifests itself. Currently the term "affective disorders" is employed to describe the conditions in which depression is a main or associated feature. As suggested by Winokur ("Depression: The Clinical Perspective," *Practical Psychiatry*), there is a family of disorders that may be covered by the term "primary depression." In these problems the subjective distress of the individual is thought to derive fundamentally from biological or physiological causes. Reactions to a particular loss or to other negative incidents are considered "secondary depressions." The primary affective disorders include two main subdivisions: manic-depressive, or bipolar, disease and depressive, or unipolar, disease. In the first instance there are sharply definable alterations in mood, with swings from mania to depression. In depressive disease there is no history of any manic, or hyperactive, episodes. The task of distinguishing between these and planning for proper treatment is one for the professional in the mental health field. The nonprofessional needs a much more general idea of depression and its role as an indicator of an impending or actual crisis.

Workers who must handle emergencies should, however, be aware of the other entities in which depressive symptoms appear. These include depressions that are secondary to some other serious psychiatric problem, depressions associated with physical illness, and depression as a characteristic of the mourning process. It is not uncommon, for example, to detect depression in individuals who are in the withdrawal process from alcohol or drugs. Depressive symptoms may also be a side-effect from the use of a prescribed medication. In such situations the symptoms ordinarily disappear with the passage of time after the usage of the drug is discontinued. Many physical illnesses, even before they are correctly diagnosed, may give rise to classic symptoms of depression. For the emergency worker, these distinctions suggest the care that must be exercised in coming to conclusions about the nature of the depressive complaints, especially under the pressure of a crisis, when partial or distorted information, like the first news headlines about a disaster, is likely to accompany them.

What We Need To Know

Some things can be said in general about depression that may be helpful to nonprofessional counselors. Depressive symptoms demand our sensitive attention because they may be warning flags about critical life events. To what do we direct our attention? Perhaps this question may be phrased another way. How can we be sure that what we are observing is not just an example of up-and-down emotions that are common to all human beings? We must test this situation, as a baker does a loaf of bread, to sense its texture. If, for example, the individual has experienced a major change in mood, that is, if it is clearly a break in his or her normal pattern of reactions, than it cannot be shrugged off as an everyday variant.

We should pay attention, in other words, if someone who is not ordinarily a whiner begins to complain regularly about the problems of life or the fact that it is no longer worth living. People who experience a real depression frequently claim that nothing seems to make any difference to them anymore. Their spirits cannot be revived by urging them to seek some kind of distraction or vacation. It really does not help them very much to buck them up with pep talks or to encourage them on to renewed efforts. They are too flat, too immersed in a twilight of gloom even to smile at such suggestions. People can recover from feeling sorry for themselves; but this is not true of people in the grip of depression. Their world is without relief, with little hope of dawn, and they speak of their personal darkness in a very discouraged fashion.

SIGNS

Nonprofessionals should familiarize themselves with the classic signs that are ordinarily coupled with depression of this more serious nature. What are some of these indications? The vegetative signals can be observed easily. These include the sleep pattern of the individual. A person who is depressed may sleep very little or far more than usual. A disturbance in either direction may indicate some problem in this area. Naturally, everybody can wake up early at times or find it difficult to go to sleep at night. We have grown familiar with such occurrences and realize that for reasonably normal people they usually point to some distress in our lives. How, then, can we differentiate these rather normal reactions from the depressive symptoms of sleep disturbance that should alert us to a critical moment in an individual's life?

The duration of the complaint is an important dimension to observe. Some consistency of troubled patterns over a period of ten days or two weeks suggest that a serious problem underlies thse reported difficulties. Change in appetite suggests the same. If the individual departs from the normal pattern of eating, either by excessive or lessened appetite, that tells the same story. Our eating habits are very sensitive to mood changes. It is no accident that we speak of not being able to swallow or stomach certain people or events or that, in our enthusiasm, we feel like eating somebody else up. We should always pay attention when someone presents consistent digestive complaints because any departure from regularity in bodily functions over a sustained period of time usually provides a clue about possible serious depressive problems.

OTHER SYMPTOMS

Depression also reveals itself through evidence of psychomotor retardation, which refers to any slowness in general movement and thinking that represents a change rather than merely the temporary difficulty that may accompany some other illness. Psychomotor retardation may, for example, be observed in people who simply cannot seem to get themselves together. They fail to organize their day or to achieve the goals that they were previously able to move toward without any serious difficulty. Any change in the sharpness of a person's responses may point to the possibility of an underlying depressive process. When, for example, we observe that people are easily distracted or unable to concentrate over long periods, we may wish to investigate further to see whether, in combination with other signs, these provide evidence of the onset of a crisis that is projecting itself in depression.

WHAT IS IMPORTANT?

The nature of the crisis associated with depression may be suicidal. We must be alert, then, to any tendencies to self-depreciation. Truly depressed persons can find no good in themselves and constantly blame themselves for things that happen; they seem unable to give themselves credit for any good that they may have accomplished. They can see only the dark side of their lives and often are obsessively concerned with their guilt. While we all may regret certain things we have done, we can easily differentiate this from the constant worry over very minor things that frequently characterizes the depressed person.

Nonprofessionals are frequently tempted, as are all persons, to respond with old-fashioned reassurance in the face of some temporary mood dislocation. We do it with ourselves and with those with whom we are familiar; when somebody comes to us with what appears to be a similar reaction, we use the same strategy. A principal sign that a crisis is unfolding is the fact that such reassurance simply does not work. Self-centered helpers may not notice this. They may merely become irritated when their advice is not followed. They become frustrated as they discover that they are repeating encouraging advice over and over and yet, despite all their urgings, the person is simply not pulling himself or herself together. Here the frustrated reactions of those standing by actually provide us with a sign that the person is suffering from something more than a passing difficulty. This is precisely the kind of signal that the nonprofessional should be able to pick up and interpret accurately. In fact it may be more significant than many other indications. The depressive bulge in a person's life affects others, distorting their lives by involving them in excessive efforts to encourage the person at the center of attention. We can read the problem person in these very reactions; they are like a rader screen outline.

What Can We Do?

If reassurances do not help, what can we do if a depression signals a crisis? Nonprofessionals need to respond not by taking on the treatment of such persons but by understanding how to get treatment for them. If our line of work may bring us in contact with persons suffering incipient crises marked by depression, then we should work out in advance the steps to take in order to make effective referrals for them. If we have not thought of referrals, we have not thought through our role as emergency helpers. If we do not know how to make referrals, we have not adequately rehearsed our role in assisting others who give signals of serious depression.

We should acquaint ourselves with the resources in our particular environment, such as the emergency room of the local hospital, counseling resources available through various social agencies, and the names of individual therapists who have the training and experience to give professional treatment to persons with depressive difficulties.

If we are involved in a developing crisis heralded by depression, we should first obtain the name of the individual's family doctor. This can be done when we record the individual's life history. The family doctor is a first-line source of referral. We can almost always be sure that he or she will be acquainted with a full range of colleagues who can assist the person who is under stress. The family doctor often serves as an anchor and as a mediator who can be extremely helpful in consolidating and working through the crisis situation with an individual and family members.

Why Shouldn't We Try?

Most helpers sincerely want to try to do something constructive for others. Why do we urge so much caution when we deal with indications of serious depression? Because it is easy to do the wrong thing. Amateur therapists, or those with a little training in something like client-centered therapy, are not able to help depressive patients because they are not thoroughly trained in the sensitive and difficult task of establishing genuine relationships with those suffering from this particular problem. Reaching the depressed person demands a level of clinical acumen and skill that is generally beyond the range of the nonprofessional. Trying to reach the feelings of the depressed individual and to reflect them, as amateur counselors do, seems to be easy. But this involvement of the helper is on a rather superficial level, usually imitating proper therapy, and may therefore cause difficulties. Engaging in counselinglike work is not really helpful to the patient, and in the long run, it is not helpful to the emergency worker either. Beginning to help and then getting lost is discouraging to emergency helpers, and after a certain number of such experiences, they begin to feel that they are failures at what they are trying to do. Such helpers cannot seem to reach or deal effectively with the very people they are so highly motivated to help. The art involved in making a true psychological contact requires more training than we can expect of people who, in an emergency, are asked only to make the initial response simply and directly. The emergency worker's task is to bridge the chasm of the emergency, not to provide ongoing psychotherapy; this bridging is in itself a splendid achievement. Nonprofessionals should not burden themselves with attempts at treatment that may only make them feel that they are failing.

First Steps

Emergency workers need, of course, to make a judgment, at least a rough one, about the nature of the difficulty with which they are dealing. Although they may be sophisticated enough to differentiate the various forms of depression with complete accuracy, they need also to be able to make a decision about the depression's seriousness and depth, as a first step toward referral for other treatment. To this end, crisis counselors can use the opportunity of the interview to take the soundings that are necessary to make such a decision.

While they participate in the interview, they also observe, as the old psychological adage goes. In addition, they need to handle themselves in a manner that will both assist the other person and at the same time facilitate the interview process. It is obviously a time for a serious and concerned manner; the meeting with a depressed person is not an occasion for light banter, jokes, or other activities supposedly aimed at achieving rapport.

Closely allied to this is the need to be supportive rather than challenging. A district attorney–like mode of inquiry will almost surely upset the depressed person and make the interview more difficult.

It is best to proceed at the depressed individual's pace, which is ordinarily slower than usual; that, in fact, is a sign of depression, as we have previously noted. We should try to calibrate our responses and our demeanor to this blunted pace, making sure that our own needs to get this case settled, or to make a diagnosis, are well in hand. If our ability to help depends on making a quick and gratifying contact with the other person, we will be frustrated in trying to assay the condition of the depressed individual. He or she is remote, at a distance from relationship, and we must both tolerate and evaluate this nonengagement as a symptom rather than as a barrier that we must dextrously and immediately hurdle.

CONDUCTING THE INTERVIEW

While in other situations many helpers adopt a somewhat expectant attitude, one that generates pressure on the person being seen, that is not the strategy of choice in these circumstances. We should be willing to take more than the usual amount of responsibility for the interview, both in placing the questions and in reinforcing its cohesive and purposive structure. We want to be active, that is, to move ahead with a systematic inquiry that not only yields information but also gives the patient something to do. The latter approach is far superior to conducting the interview as a kind of puzzle, which only makes the person feel less, rather than more, competent.

We must also be prepared for emotional expressions, such as sighing and crying, from depressed persons. When these do occur, they often point to key incidents and issues involved in the development of their depression, but we should not be surprised if they are absent. Nor should we consider their absence a sign that no depression exists. Severely depressed persons may not cry at all, and persons who have finally made the decision to commit suicide may not seem depressed at all; the gloom may have lifted after the act of decision. If there are tears, we should not falsely attempt to stop them; we should let them fall, allowing the person to see that we can accept his or her distress.

As the interview progresses we watch for signals about the precipitant of the depression; we try to get some sense of the depression's duration, whether there have been previous episodes and something about their intensity and how and where they were treated. At the same time that we're doing this, we are also trying to get a sense of the person's general style—of the way he or she responds to and manages problems—and an idea of the resources that are available to support the person through this difficult time. We may have to listen carefully to pick up the anger that is so often present and so often denied by depressed persons. As we gather information and observe the psychological style of the individual, we gradually get a sense of the texture of the experience and can begin to make some tentative conclusions about where it may fit in the family of depressive problems.

The evaluation of suicide risk in the depressed individual will be discussed in the next chapter.

For Further Reading

Ayd, F. J. *Recognizing the Depressed Patient*. New York: Grune and Stratton, 1961.

Beck, Aaron T. *Depression: Clinical, Experimental and Theoretical Aspects*. New York: Harper and Row, 1967.

Becker, Joseph. *Affective Disorders*. New Jersey: General Learning Press, 1977.

Friedman, R. J., and Katz, M. M. (eds.) *The Psychology of Depression: Contemporary Theory and Research*. Washington, DC: V. H. Winston & Sons, 1974.

Miller, W. R. "Psychological Deficit in Depression." *Psychological Bulletin* 82 (1975), pp. 233–60.

Winokur, G., "The Types of Affective Disorders." *Journal of Nervous and Mental Disease* 156 (1973), pp. 82–96.

SIX

Suicidal Emergencies

THERE is no emergency more dramatic or more draining than that which surrounds the threat of, or attempt at, self-destruction. The non-professional counselor may become involved in such a crisis at any of a number of potential entry points, and, therefore, a sensitive and common-sense assessment of what is going on is absolutely necessary. Nonprofessionals, for short periods of time at least, may find themselves the only ones who can make judgments on the dangers of the crisis and the actions that should be taken.

Suicide has been discussed extensively in popular culture in recent years. There has been a measure of romanticization of the act of taking one's life, as indeed there has been of death itself. There is very little that is truly new in this development, since fads and fancies about death—cast now as enchanter, now as reaper—have been recycled throughout history. On the other hand, the mood of attraction to death, to the dark at the end of it all that beckons us mysteriously toward it, is being balanced by a new sensitivity to death's realities and by a readiness to understand and respond to suicidal threats and gestures. While all this goes on, and in the midst of the veritable inundation of literature on death and dying in offices and schools, the emergency counselor is preoccupied with his or her own main work, ordinarily too busy for either the metaphysics or the mechanics of such discussions. And, as a matter of fact, the crisis counselor does not have to take part in or necessarily know much about any of these issues in order to be helpful. It is perfectly acceptable to be on the margins of the death-fascinated society; in many situations such a stance may prove beneficial, because no abstract discussions will impede the actions that have to be taken.

43

SUICIDE SIGNS

Depression, which has already been discussed, is obviously an indicator to which we must be carefully attuned in evaluating the suicide potential of individuals who may come or be referred to us. At least half "of all suicides are suffering from an episode of a primary affective disorder (depression) when they take their lives," according to G. E. Murphy. ("Suicide and Attempted Suicide," *Hospital Practice*). An overlapping group, alcoholics, accounts for another quarter of all suicides. An ability to interpret correctly the depressive symptoms previously described is therefore essential to the counselor who, by whatever route, intervenes.

A NOSTALGIC QUALITY

Prudence is a word that is hardly ever used in the contemporary world; indeed, it has a quaint ring to it and the surprising pungency of nostalgia. Still, it remains a significant if not indispensable characteristic for all counselors, whether professionals or not. No quality of judgment is more essential in dealing with crises in which suicidal potential is to be evaluated.

Prudence can roughly be equated with clinical judgment, that amalgam of training, experience, and innate sensibility that the physician or other helper employs in diagnosing an individual and developing a treatment plan. It is the same quality used by farmers as they read the skies to set the moment for the harvest or by the widest range of people, from artists to teachers, in dealing with the concerns about which they truly know something. They never apply external criteria blindly or impersonally. Sound clinical judgment is a profoundly human attribute; it is accurate knowledge seasoned with personal wisdom, and nothing is more crucial in making a judgment about an individual's potential for suicide.

One cannot, for example, take the sociological categories of high- and low-risk suicide potential, match the person in crisis to them, and then make a decision one way or another. While such categories are extremely valuable sources of information and should be factored into any evaluation of suicide risk, their effective use depends on our capacity to sense and explore accurately the inner struggle of the affected person. Beebe ("Evaluation of the Suicidal Patient," in *Psychiatric Treatment Crisis/Clinic/Consultation*) emphasizes the need for a "feeling" appraisal, for only then can one "counsel survival convincingly." Otherwise we run the risk of being "just another stranger telling the patient how to feel" (p. 20).

Obviously, such counsel for a "feeling" evaluation requires some tempering by the quality we call prudence lest the nonprofessional become unwittingly involved in transference-countertransference phenomena, with results that may be confusing if not harmful to both the counselor and the affected person. It is clear, however, that we have to be close enough to persons in crisis to see them clearly and to communicate our human concern to them. Balance, the core of prudence and clinical judgment, remains essential. It is this balance that leads nonprofessionals to a calm espousal of the basic principle in working with crises marked by suicide potential.

BASIC PRINCIPLE

Most experts in the field agree that we should take seriously any individual who either threatens suicide or makes a suicidal gesture. This does not mean, of course, that we drop a net on them immediately or become overdramatic in our approach. Being serious means that we take prudent and unhurried steps to evaluate the nature of the suicide threat. Here, of course, is precisely where we must draw on our store of information and meld that with our clinical sensitivity—and that includes our feeling responses to the individual—in order to make a good human judgment on what steps should next be taken.

What informational materials or clues can prove helpful to us in this process? If, for example, the person fits into that section of the demographic analysis of suicide potential that is clearly high-risk, we want to incorporate this information with appropriate concern into our perspective of judgment. This is the type of information we take very seriously.

For example, if the person is socially unattached—if there are no close family connections and little evidence of significant social participation—we do not treat his or her suicide potential casually. As noted in the literature, such risks may be modified by external conditions. Peacetime may find such persons more adrift and isolated than ever, while periods of war and disruption, with their increased tension, frequently change the social situation, so that the person is brought into the community group more effectively. Research conducted in Belfast, for example, has shown that the incidence of depression was less in that city than in peaceful County Down. The interplay of such factors must be appreciated by counselors because it is out of just such a mix of factors that sound clinical judgments are formed.

If the individual has an alcoholic problem, then we would, without needing a great deal of additional evidence, weight the suicidal risk in the depressed person much more seriously. Fox claims that the suicide rate for alcoholics is fifty-five times the national average. Depression and alcoholism frequently overlap, and since between them they account for three-quarters of all suicides, we should pay careful attention when this combination of symptoms is present.

As to depression itself, we must not concentrate only on its gloomiest phases. Suicide is sometimes attempted when the depression is apparently improving, or when, in other words, the individual claims to be feeling better. Beebe suggests that this may be accounted for in one of two ways (p. 31): Such persons may not possess enough physical or psychological energy to kill themselves while they are deeply depressed. Reduced movement and lowered energy are characteristic of extremely depressed individuals. When the depression lifts, the surge of returning energy may fuel their will to act. On the other hand, it is possible that depressed patients, once they are back out into the light, dread the return to their darkened state so much that they then commit suicide. The depressed person often suicides in the convalescent stage of illness, while the schizophrenic more often attempts it during an early stage of the psychosis.

The previously depressed person may, in fact, seem almost cheerful just before the suicide. This kind of freedom seems to follow after the decision, and their apparently positive mood is a sign that their plaguing ambivalence has at last been resolved. They are finally at peace because the last act has been played out and they are simply waiting for the curtains to close.

We must be alert to any history of previous suicide attempts. Nothing tells us about the future more clearly than the pattern of the past. Any previous suicide attempt tells us that this possibility should be taken very seriously in the present. It is a major clue about the seriousness of the condition.

WHERE ELSE TO LOOK

Other flares that speak clearly of the ominous state of things may also be found in the person's life history. Has there been a loss or the serious threat of a loss recently? Suicidal people don't fool around; they act under the impact of adverse events. Health problems, serious or perceived as such, may portend suicide, especially in older people. So too may life events such as indictment, imprisonment, or financial ruin. Beebe points out that social disgrace need not require a crowd. Strip away a person's defenses, so that their ordinary supports are gone, and they may well attempt suicide. This could happen in a classroom, a closed office, or in an ill-starred encounter-group experience. Such events may well precipitate serious psychological emergencies, and we should not underestimate their destructive potential.

Just as disruptive civil conditions may reduce depression and decrease suicide potential, so, on the other hand, may a drifting and languid life, with no observable direction or purpose, make detached and floating persons more vulnerable to suicide. Self-destruction ends their boredom or disappointment, or their melancholy realization that they cannot now undo what they have already done or experienced. Persons in such a state have, in effect, lost their reasons to live; they need a rekindling of meaning in order to help them get through their critical period.

Obviously there will be some gradations of danger in individual cases. The person who has spent the last of his or her money, called a friend to say good-bye, and left the house unlocked is clearly at much greater risk of suicide then is the person who has no serious suicide plan at all. Coming to a judgment in each situation is necessary, however, if the emergency is to be managed. We need to do something in response to the escalating dangers before the drama moves quickly to a close.

COUNSELING SUGGESTIONS

We need resolution and firmness along with our warm concern as we deal with the troubled person. This is not a time for heightening ambivalence with open-ended questions. We want to capitalize on their trust in us in order to offer them our strength, so that during the crisis we can become a surrogate for their wills. We also need to be readily and easily available and to involve others who can help. We do not leave seriously suicidal people alone or on their own for long periods of time.

In speaking with a person who is a serious suicidal risk, we may endeavor, as MacKinnon and Michels suggest (*The Psychiatric Interview in Clinical Practice*), to help the individual "express in the interview the same emotions that the suicide will symbolize." Then, the person's own controls will be able to operate more effectively, and the need for committing suicide will be lessened.

A PSYCHOLOGICAL VIEW

In a brilliant and helpful essay, Edwin S. Schneidman offers a theory of suicide with which those in emergency work should become familiar ("A Psychologic Theory of Suicide," *Psychiatric Annals*). Focusing on the "rather suddenly executed suicidal act," he notes that, characteristically, such actions are (1) judged "by the suicidal person to be fatal," usually entailing "jumping, shooting, burning or hanging," (2) such decisions are ordinarily sudden, perhaps "a few days or even just minutes before the event," and (3) these suicidal actions are "not directly communicated to others."

He suggests three main components, or "ingredients," plus a spark to ignite them in all such cases: (1) heightened inimicality or self-hate, (2) exacerbation of perturbation or psychological imbalance, (3) progressive constriction of intellectual focus, or narrowing of the mind's content, and (4) the notion of cessation, or, as Schneidman puts it, "the insight that it is possible to stop consciousness and put an end to suffering,' which is the spark that sets off the explosion of suicide.

WHAT DO THESE MEAN?

Schneidman speaks of the "inimicality thrust" in individuals and suggests that it can be evaluated according to the number of acts that the subject is performing against his or her best interests. Roughly speaking, then, this characteristic is revealed in persons who exceed the usual limits of their self-defeating behaviors. We all recognize that we can hurt ourselves in various ways, even when these are rather small, as through smoking or eating. Other persons regularly lead lives marked by harmful excess. The warning signal is sounded when there is an increase of such activities in a person's life and activities.

Perturbation is used by Schneidman to describe how "disturbed, 'shook-up,' ill at ease, or mentally upset a person is." He notes that there are dangers in "trying to be too specific" about this quality, warning against trying "to tie all suicide to depression, which is only one form of perturbation." Schneidman quotes Henry A. Murray's analysis of emotional states reported in men who committed suicide in Veterans' Administration hospitals. These states included (1) pitiful forlornness, deprivation, distress, and grief; (2) extrapunitiveness or blaming, as well as anger and physical aggression; (3) intrapunitiveness or remorse and guilt or depression; (4) leaving or desertion behavior; and (5) no emotional response at all, a way, as he notes, of "being dead to the world" (cf. *Essays in Self-Destruction*).

Constricted or narrowed thinking suggests that the corridor of thought is so shadowed that one's "ordinary thoughts and loves and feelings and responsibilities are simply not available to consciousness." Persons on the edge of suicide cannot use their past or its memories and relationships to prevent the suicide because they are so intensely focused on the present painful emotion.

When the previously mentioned emotional states are combined with this notion of the cessation of consciousness, or the real possibility of putting a stop to pain, then the situation becomes lethal. As Schneidman observes, "What is especially tragic is that this idea of cessation is often not communicated by suicidal persons. . . . The idea of cessation, because it is so dramatic and so breathtaking and so dangerous, is often kept a secret from the therapist. It follows from this that any talk of committing suicide must be investigated very carefully and very seriously."

Once we have assessed the suicide threat according to these norms, we must work "to reduce the inimicality and perturbation in the patient." That is the quality that we can deal with most straightforwardly by reassurance and by our own strong and dependable presence.

FURTHER QUESTIONS

In addition to carefully reading the combination of signals described above, we might also note whether the individual has suffered a loss or expressed any other serious problems recently. When we have a conviction that the person exhibits all the signs of suicide, including the talk of ending it in one way or another, we should not hesitate to ask whether they have, in fact, made any plans in this regard. Some people are reluctant to do this, fearing that they will make things worse, when actually such an inquiry only yields information to us but also offers relief to the troubled individual. Just as we must lay to rest the notion that those who speak of suicide never commit it, so too we must put aside our own uneasiness in favor of sensible inquiry about whether they have procured the means or have worked out, even in general, any plans for suicide.

We have to get at the hard facts of the case. We must not confuse suicidal thoughts with a suicidal plan. More than half of us have had suicidal thoughts; the thought of suicide does not by itself indicate that a person is truly a serious risk. The situation is far different for the person who knows just what they want to do and how to do it. What are the individual's feelings about these plans? Can we discern the meaning that suicide may have in the life of this person? Such questions help us to clarify our picture of the person's intentions and to evaluate the nature of the suicidal potential.

Caution is advised about getting the person into philosophical arguments about the situation. We do not wish to mobilize their argumentative strengths; we want to search out and help them to express more positive emotions. What, for example, are the things that they have valued in life, what are the things that made it important or sweet to them (*op. cit.,* p. 208)?

Nor do we wish to relieve them of all responsibility by claiming that we will save them by taking care of everything. That may be a bigger promise than we can keep and may cause the person to relax their inner controls even further. We want to reinforce what strengths we can find, while we move toward referral to competent medical or psychological help. Obviously, a serious suicidal crisis will offer a test of our referral skills as well as our knowledge of what agencies, hospitals, or mental health experts we can call on to accept the referral process.

SOME ADDED SUGGESTIONS

Common-sense steps should follow the preliminary judgment that the situation is critical. We should see to it that the means of suicide are removed or that access to them is adequately controlled during the period of emergency. This includes guns, medications, or unattended presence in locations such as the upper floors of a building from which a suicide attempt might easily be made. We should tell the person what we plan to do to help, neither in panic nor with rash promises; calmness, as frequently mentioned, coupled with firmness, can put some spine into a dangerously sagging condition. Make sure that our communication with the person is as open as possible; agree with them on a definite next meetingtime if a referral cannot be effected immediately.

Before contacting family members or friends we should tell the person or seek his or her permission. This frees us from trying to reach others in roundabout ways or through ruses. It also involves the suicidal patient and makes our role as well as our intentions clear. We cannot be bound to silence or to a species of pseudoconfidentiality at such a time, and while we seek the individual's permission, we do not want to be put off by some rigidity or effort to manipulate us. We should contact without delay a responsible member of the person's family. If the individual is already in treatment with a professional, then we are ethically and morally obliged to contact that person if we feel that we are faced with a serious danger.

The latter situation is not an uncommon one for nonprofessionals. Their help is sought at times for the very reason that the affected individual wants to avoid facing or working through some psychological difficulty with the professional they are already seeing. Clergy and teachers are particularly vulnerable to patients who wish to use them to manipulate a therapeutic relationship to which the patients are already a part. It is never a good idea to ignore professionals who already have some responsibility for the person with whom we are dealing; our best service to everyone concerned is to inform such persons and make them part of our response as quickly as possible. They can then assume their responsibilities for decisions about hospitalization and continuing treatment.

For Further Reading

Alvarez, A. *The Savage God.* New York: Random House, 1972.

Beebe, John E., III. "Evaluation of the Suicidal Patient." In *Psychiatric Treatment Crisis/Clinic/Consultation* (C. P. Rosenbaum and J. G. Beebe, III, eds.). New York: McGraw-Hill, 1975.

Fox, Ruth. *Alcoholism—Behavioral Research, Therapeutic Approaches.* New York: Springer Publishing Co., 1967

Freud, Sigmund. "Mourning and Melancholia." In *The Complete Works of Sigmund Freud.* London: Hogarth Press, 1957.

Litman, Robert. "Management of Acutely Suicidal Patients in Medical Practice." *California Medicine* 104 (1966), pp. 168–74.

MacKinnon, Roger A., and Michels, Robert. *The Psychiatric Interview in Clinical Practice.* Philadelphia: W. B. Saunders & Co., 1974, p. 206.

Murphy, G. E. "Suicide and Attempted Suicide." *Hospital Practice,* Nov. 1977, p. 73.

Ringel, Irwin, M. D. "The Pre-Suicidal Syndrome." *Suicide and Life-Threatening Behavior* 6:3 (Fall 1976), pp. 131–49.

Robins, Eli, et al. "The Communication of Suicidal Intent: A Study of 134 Consecutive Cases of Successful (Completed) Suicide." *American Journal of Psychiatry* 115 (1959), pp. 724–33.

Schneidman, Edwin, and Farberon, Norman (eds.). *Clues for Suicide.* New York: McGraw-Hill, 1957.

Schneidman, Edwin (ed.). *Essays in Self-Destruction.* New York: Science House, 1967.

SEVEN

The Right to Know

THE idea that everyone possesses a right to know even the inside details of incidents that come to public attention has been thoroughly drilled into the heads of most Americans. Indeed, it is repeated so often through various aspects of the media that a person tempted to object to this philosophy may experience conditioned feelings of guilt and so be compelled to put the objection aside. While there may be many instances in which this maxim can be applied, it remains true that one is not a Fascist if one registers some exceptions to this rule.

This has special relevance in the field of crisis counseling. Ethical codes already exist for psychiatrists and psychologists that insist on the confidential nature of helping relationships. Indeed, the public naturally expects that whatever individuals divulge to therapists, or therapistlike figures, will remain confidential. Moral codes place expectations on all of us regarding secrets or the use of the other materials that may come into our possession as a result of the positions of confidence that we hold. At times the very nature of this information impels us to keep it secret. Despite all this, there has been an extended debate about the nature of therapist confidentiality that, over the past few years, has found a counterpoint in judicial decisions regarding cases of confidentiality. Indeed, state legislatures across the country have even prescribed, in rather diverse ways, the exceptions to confidentiality for therapists. While the nonprofessional caught up in an emergency cannot be expected to remember all of these things and may have to rely on common sense, it is prudent to review some of the principles and examples for which they may be called into question.

A TRUSTED POSITION

The nonprofessional helpers to whom persons caught up in crises turn almost always have an established relationship of trust with them. This may be because such trust is accorded to every member of his or her profession, as is generally thought to be the case with members of the clergy. Teachers, lawyers, and many others share deeply in this, and any professional who projects a genuinely trustworthy personality will be the recipient of confidences at times of emergency. It has also been noted that this delegation of trust provides a basis for a successful intervention: Since the subjects already trust us, they will be willing to follow our suggestions.

There are other sides to this question of trust, however, and if we are associated even on an irregular basis with emergencies, it is helpful to know and to reflect on their personal implications. We do not ordinarily have time in the midst of crises to entertain a dialectic on our ethical obligations.

The typical emergency situation presents the emergency worker with a privileged view of a cross-section of the life of an individual or a family. Not only do helpers see the event at the heart of the crisis, whether this be an attempted suicide, an alcoholic binge, or some unusual sexual behavior, but they also see the connective tissues of related life experiences and conditions. We may learn about things that, outside the family circle, are well-kept secrets. If we cut across any individual's life we would be bound to find a certain number of surprises—that a drinking problem has existed for a long time, that someone is illegitimate, that someone else has been in jail—and a dizzying array of the other all-too-human truths. Even undertakers make discoveries in moments of heightened vulnerability that they must keep to themselves.

This, in fact, is the point: Emergencies may be short in duration, but they can yield a disproportionately rich array of facts that demand confidentiality. Approaching crises with this understanding both enables us to anticipate the surprises and to handle them prudently. We deserve trust only so long as we are able to keep trust alive. In this matter the nonprofessional follows the model of professional helpers.

QUESTIONS FOR PROFESSIONALS

If following the model of professional behavior seems straightforward, we soon discover the complications, thick as spider webs, that surround this issue for them at this time. While confidentiality has been accepted as a general condition of the helping professions, there have been disputes about whether and when this can be qualified, in view, for example, of possible harm to third parties.

A recent study has also revealed that most professionals do not understand the difference between the meaning of confidentiality and privileged communication. These are not interchangeable notions, and emergency helpers should understand that. Confidentiality refers to the general ethic of professional relationships that forbids the counselor from revealing any of the material learned in the relationship without the permission of the client. Some say there are other circumstances that excuse the helper from confidentiality as well.

Privileged communication is much narrower in meaning and refers to the protection of material from disclosure in the courtroom. It is a legally determined idea that is regulated by statutes that vary from state to state. Many professionals who have claimed the notion of privileged communication have been surprised to discover that it did not apply to them. This is because legislatures have passed so many exceptions to the rule of privilege. In *Psychiatry and Law,* R. Slovenko writes that such statutes "for all practical purposes, render the privilege a nullity". The same survey disclosed that many professionals think that privilege protects them when, in fact, it does not, and many others fail to appreciate the distinction between this and the general idea of confidentiality. In any case, no crisis worker should think that some vague invocation of privilege will completely free him or her from divulging information or even notes that may be demanded in later legal proceedings.

The fact that so many exceptions have compromised the absolute quality of client-helper communications has led many observers to demand that counselors respect the patient's revelations without any conditions or exceptions. This is an extreme position, but it is supported by those who are convinced that confidentiality is the very foundation of any therapeutic relationship and therefore demands an unyielding principle. Still others add the argument that one profession cannot allow another profession (the law) to determine what shall be made public and what shall not. Those who take this stance are particularly aware of the sensitive nature of the therapeutic relationship and of the ways in which, through the law, a therapist may be subtly manipulated and lose control of this relationship. This may happen, for example, if a client uses the law to force a therapist to reveal information about his or her spouse or married life that may be relevant in a later divorce case.

While making room for these positions, others hold that exceptions to the rule of absolute confidentiality must be made when the health or welfare of a third party would otherwise be subject to injury. For example, if a helper learns from a person in a crisis that they plan to murder someone, he or she would be free of the ordinary strictures of confidentiality in order to alert that person about the danger.

THE LAW STEPS IN

The law may contravene a profession's ethical principles by statutes that are contrary to them. Thus, in some states, helpers would violate a law if they did not report certain information that came to them confidentially. In a celebrated case in California, a psychologist was found liable for not reporting a death threat made by a client about a female student even though he did notify the campus police (*Tarasoff v. The Regents of California*).

Almost every state has passed a statute requiring helpers and others to report any information they gain about child abuse to the police. A recent study revealed that many therapists, even though they were full-time professionals, did not know the requirements of the law and that many of them, responding to a hypothetical case, would be willing to break the law in order to protect the confidential nature of the relationship. The authors noted:

This suggests the complexity of the problem. Negative attitude toward the law appears to be an equal, if not a greater, problem than ignorance of the law . . . There is the negative attitude toward infringing on the rights of an individual, the fear of retaliation from the client. . . . In addition, there are basic philosophical differences that inhibit adherence to this law. Many of the laws requiring child abuse reporting seem to be punitively oriented, as evidenced by the fact that they specify the police as the agency to which reports should be sent. Most mental health professionals, however, are therapeutically oriented; as a result, they may consider interfering with the therapeutic relationship in order to report child abuse as having more damaging consequences than helpful ones. (Swoboda, Elwork, Sales, and Levine, "Knowledge and Compliance with Privileged Communication and Child-Abuse Reporting Laws," *Professional Psychology*).

In a microcosmic way the differing approaches to the statutes concerning child abuse present us with a sense of the conflict and uncertainty that surround questions of confidentiality for professionals. Nonprofessionals need to think out these issues and be prepared to follow consistent principles during and after their involvement in a crisis situation.

COMMON SENSE

Common sense probably provides the best baseline for decisions about matters of confidentiality in emergencies. And the basic principle is to say as little as possible to as few people as possible regardless of how serious or dramatic the situation may be. Let us consider some examples that will be familiar to nonprofessional helpers.

A priest in a large religious order is asked by his superior to go pick up another member of the same order who has been arrested in a nearby town. The assigned priest carries out the task, discovering in the process of paying bail that the arrested colleague has been arrested before on charges of shoplifting. On the way home it becomes clear that the priest who had been arrested is in the midst of a crisis in his life; he confides that he has had severe problems for years that he had always managed to hush up, and asks for help. Upon their return, the helping priest is asked by his religious superior for a complete account of what transpired.

The questions here are obvious. Was the priest sent as a kind of parole officer or as an extension of the superior's administrative authority? Was he a nonprofessional counselor and did he assume a burden of confidentiality when the arrested priest confided in him and asked for further help? How much is he free to reveal, or should he reveal anything?

These and similar questions could be asked in this situation and, transposing the circumstances slightly, in many other settings besides that of Catholic religious life. But in fact, confidentiality is frequently broken in just these circumstances because there is no questioning of the authority's expectations. Most superiors, or other authorities, would, however, be reasonable if the helper explained that not everything could be discussed and that, for the good of the individual, arrangements for further help should be made without additional questioning at this time. If the priest in question is capable of it, he might be urged to take responsibility for explaining something of his plight. This is not always possible, however, since in such an emergency the principal character may be too anxious or upset to bare his or her secrets to those in authority.

Similar problems may face companies that have provided access to medical and other help for their employees during times of stress. The company executive or the aide who makes the contact and the referral is, for all intents and purposes, a crisis counselor, and loyalty to the principles of therapy may take precedence over loyalty to company superiors.

Cases like these arise in every business and institution in the land, and often the same people are asked to handle them. They may, as personnel directors, have explicit responsibility for dealing with such situations. They should think out their position beforehand and not allow themselves to be pressured into uncomfortable and highly compromised situations in which they can only lose their credibility as helpers and administrators. Those who handle personnel problems in any school or organization need some agreed-upon leeway for judgment in emergencies as well as the independent authority to make arrangements for referrals or other follow-up. The exploding emergency is not the background for establishing one's rights and responsibilities as a manager of such problems.

"Less is usually more" serves as a rule of thumb about communicating material that falls under the heading of confidential. There is always time to reveal it later, but, as common sense tells us, there is no way to retrieve it once it has been broadcast within any social system. Obviously, situations that involve potential suicides or homicides require us to act swiftly and to make the communications that are necessary for the well-being of others. There are, however, a host of lesser events—and they are far more common for the crisis counselor—that require informed discretion.

THE EFFORT TO BIND THE HELPER

It takes a sensitive and strong person to appreciate the demands of confidentiality and to separate these from the manipulations of clients, who, as we have previously discussed, may attempt to swear the helper to some form of secrecy that is premature and inappropriate. The difference involved here comes down to the question of whether we remain in charge or else allow ourselves to become the agent of the affected person's wishes or manipulations.

Such efforts at manipulation are characteristic of certain troubled persons, such as alcoholics or others who have adjusted to life and to their problems by employing defenses that consistently play people off against each other. They try to incorporate anyone who helps them into this pattern, and, in the heart of even drastic emergencies, they do not change very much. We need enough distance from manipulators to be able to remain free of their ensnaring tactics and to establish clearly our own position in the relationship without conditions being placed on it ahead of time.

THE CURIOUS

And what do emergency workers owe to those who are curious about their work, especially if it involves a situation or individual of great publicity value? Common sense tells crisis workers that they owe the cu∴≀us nothing, but it is sometimes difficult for them to act on this knowledge in practice. Here again, the need to anticipate and prepare oneself for the pressures is of paramount concern.

Why is this so? First of all, talking about difficult or trying circumstances, such as those associated with crises, is quite natural. It is one of the ways in which crisis workers deal with their own stress; it is something they may easily do when they are suffering the impact of being involved in a disaster or a poignant event of lesser proportions. We have to learn ways to manage the pressures of being involved in crises in ways other than speaking about them casually.

If we cannot be completely successful, we should avoid speaking to representatives of the media, who are by definition assigned to dig out the facts about infamous occasions and famous people. The public has little ability to defend itself against the questions of reporters. Some mystique is attached to being asked questions by them; we think we will see our names in the paper or that we will show up on the evening news. Such possibilities are hard to resist, especially when combined with the mythic principle that reporters have a right to ask us questions.

Persons who have been on the inside of any critical event have a right not to answer questions; most, in fact, have an obligation not to divulge information that will be presented for wide public consumption. Reporters will always ask us; that is the way they make their living, and crises and emergencies are always first-class news. As nonprofessionals we should not, however, report any information about the condition of people with whom we have worked, nor should we speculate in any way about their motives or any other characteristics or circumstances of the incident. Examples of failures to follow this simple principle may be viewed on television even as you are reading this.

Returning to the question of the right to know, we may as crisis counselors declare that this is notably abridged in any emergency in which we are involved. Silence very seldom increases suffering.

For Further Reading

American Psychological Association. "Ethical Standards of Psychologists." *American Psychologist* 23 (1968), pp. 357–61.

Bersoff, D. N. "Therapists as Protectors and Policemen." *Professional Psychology* 7 (1976), pp. 267–73.

Hollender, M. H. "Privileged Communication and Confidentiality." *Diseases of the Nervous System* 26 (1965), pp. 169–75.

Redlich, F., and Mollica, R. F. "Overview: Ethical Issues in Contemporary Psychiatry." *American Journal of Psychiatry* 133 (1976), pp. 1451–53.

Shah, S. A. "Privileged Communications, Confidentiality and Privacy: Privileged Communications." *Professional Psychology* 1 (1969), pp. 56–59.

————. "Privileged Communications, Confidentiality and Privacy: Confidentiality." *Professional Psychology* 2 (1970), pp. 159–64.

Slovenko, R. *Psychiatry and Law*. Boston: Little, Brown, 1973, p. 70.

Swoboda, Elwork, Sales, and Levine, "Knowledge and Compliance with Privileged Communication and Child-Abuse Reporting Laws." *Professional Psychology* 9:3, August 1978, p. 455.

Szasz, T. "The Psychiatrist as Double-Agent." *Trans-Action,* Oct. 1967, pp. 16–24.

EIGHT

Rape

HELPERS have much to understand both about those who rape and those who are raped, about their psychological states, the emotional trauma and aftermath, and the ways to deal with and assist victims or potential victims to handle this dread and hostile experience. Nonprofessional counselors may become involved in emergencies connected with rape in many ways; frequently they will be the first person called upon for emotional support and assistance after a rape, or an attempted rape, takes place. But it is also possible that one might be asked for an opinion or an evaluation of a rape problem in some public situation, such as an investigation, an educational program, or as a consultant to a legislative body or other actions that may flow from the event of a rape.

While there has been notable clarification of a number of the issues concerning rape over the last decade, ignorance, misunderstanding and misconceptions still exist, even among otherwise fairly sophisticated people. Some persons seem to prefer oversimplified ideas, such as the notion that women who get raped have been looking to get raped, and some may refuse to examine their attitudes because of unconscious conflicts or needs that they themselves do not understand. The nonprofessional who does no more than help clear up misinformation about this subject has already helped in the management of rape as an emergency.

WHAT IS RAPE?

For purposes of our reflections we accept the description of rape as forcible sexual penetration of a woman by a man under conditions of coercion and actual or implied threat of serious physical harm.

60

Homosexual rape can also occur and includes many of these same elements.

It is important to understand rape as a crime that is predominantly an expression of violent hostility toward the assaulted person. It is marked by interwoven elements of domination, degradation, and humiliation. It is therefore a mistake to conceptualize rape as an action that is motivated by sexual passion, because the objective is not primarily sexual gratification. There is, in fact, evidence of high sexual dysfunction during the act of rape that seems directly related to the hostile context of the rape situation itself (N. A. Groth, and A. W. Burgess, "Sexual Dysfunction During Rape," *New England Journal of Medicine*).

Rape cannot be understood without some appreciation of the hostile component. Simplistic interpretations not only mislead those connected with the situation but may actually interfere with the sensible and sensitive handling of it as an emergency. For example, a Wisconsin judge recently pardoned a youthful rapist with the statement that, in our culture, young girls who dressed like the victim did incite men to rape. Not only does this notion perpetuate a false interpretation, but it casts the woman in the role of the temptress. Women suffer greatly both in the way they are regarded and in the way they are treated immediately after the incident, to say nothing of the long-term effects of this punishing event.

ABOUT THE RAPIST

Understanding the personality of the man who attempts or commits rape may be particularly useful for the pastor or the educator caught up in an emergency centering around this crime. One would be naïve either to think of the rapist as merely someone too filled with youthful spirits or to accept too willingly an explanation based on one of the falsehoods that are so prevalent on the subject. Psychiatrist Richard T. Rada has observed, for example, that rapists frequently commit other types of sexual offenses, such as voyeurism or exhibitionism. "In my experience," he writes, "a careful sexual history of many rapists reveals that at least 50 percent exhibit a wide variety of sexual offenses, especially from the ages of 10 to 18 years of age . . . Mental health professionals and law enforcement officials should be alert to the importance of a careful sexual history for any adolescent or young male adult caught in the act of voyeurism or exhibitionism. Rapists have confessed that although they were apprehended for these lesser offenses, they were not questioned about their violent sexual fantasies and were too frightened or embarrassed to reveal them voluntarily" ("Commonly Asked Questions about the Rapist," *Medical Aspects of Human Sexuality*). All too often helpers may fail to suggest help at an age when it may be effective precisely because they do not explore the individual's attitudes or life history. This can be done sensitively and may not only benefit the rapist but may constitute preventive medicine against future rapes.

According to Dr. Rada, most rapists do not act impulsively. They plan their activities in great detail. They are ready to take advantage of what they may later describe as "unexpected" situations. Rada also observes that many sex offenders, including rapists, may not exhibit violence in their sexual activity with their wives or other voluntary partners. Thus many wives are amazed to learn that their husbands have been involved in such activity because they have previously betrayed no sexual violence. The husband may have beaten the wife, but the wife does not pick up sexual overtones from this. Gang rapes are frequently the activities of poorly identified males who may have a covert homosexual bond that sustains their aggressive forays against women.

Rada concludes that anyone interested in the problem of rape must be interested in the developmental histories of youths who are involved in what seem to be deviant sexual activities of a lesser degree of seriousness. This may help to identify "those who are already experiencing bizarre sexual fantasies . . . For some rapists a thorough evaluation of sexual concerns during early years might have led to appropriate intervention" (p. 56). Obviously, one does not make an automatic judgment in this regard, but nonprofessionals should not shrug off the implications of other deviant sexual emergencies with which they become associated. That is the time for an understanding exploration of the individual's psychological state, and if the nonprofessional is not up to carrying it out, he or she may at least make an intelligent and timely referral.

FACTS ABOUT RAPE

Statistics abound on the subject, and emergency workers should have some grasp of them. Even if they reveal only a partial picture, such statistics do deliver a sense of the problem's dimensions. Many experts believe that rape is still the most underreported crime in the country. Victimization surveys indicate that police statistics of 56,000 rapes reported to them each year may fall short by almost 200,000.

The report of the Law Enforcement Assistance Administration project on forcible rape (cf. *Sexuality Today,* August 21, 1978) stated that only one rape complaint out of four results in an arrest, and only one in sixty results in a conviction. Analyzing 1,200 rape complaints, they estimated that half the rapes involved strangers and another quarter were committed by men known slightly to the victims. Most of the women resisted, and most of the victims reported the crime within six hours. More than half the victims were under 21. In *Our Bodies, Ourselves* (Boston Women's Health Collective), the chapter on rape claims that half the rapes take place in the victim's own home, that the rate of rape has increased steadily over the last several years, and that 60 to 70 percent of rapes are premeditated.

REACTIONS TO RAPE

If we follow the outline suggested by Golan in *Treatment in Crisis Situations,* we can focus on the acute reaction phase, the one in which the nonprofessional counselor is most likely to become involved in this emergency. Two basic styles have been observed among victims. The first has been the "expressed style," and it is characterized by feelings of fear, anxiety, and extreme anger; these are manifested through crying, restlessness, maniclike activity, and sharp shifts in emotional reactions. The "controlled style" is exemplified by victims who mask or suppress their feelings; they appear calm and somewhat subdued.

Stressing the crisis nature of the rape, psychiatrists Carol C. Nadelson and Malkah T. Notman ("Emotional Repercussions of Rape," *Medical Aspects of Human Sexuality*) list some reactions that they feel to be almost universal among rape victims. These include "(1) disruption of normal adaptive patterns, with such symptoms as appetite and sleep disturbance, decreased attention span, and diminished level of functioning; (2) regression to a more dependent and helpless position; and (3) increased emotional susceptibility." These contain the styles of reaction mentioned by Golan and are important to understand because of the conflicts and difficulties that the victim experiences at the time of acute reaction.

For example, the victim may find it extremely difficult to talk about what has happened or may be embarrassed to have friends or family find out. Victims may only be able to reveal their experience slowly or indirectly. They may feel guilty, thinking they exercised poor judgment in some way or other and that they therefore participated in the event's development. They are concerned about publicity, pregnancy, venereal disease, or other disturbing aspects of the situation. These problems lie just beneath both the emotional and the highly controlled exterior. A sensitive helper may be able to hear the person's struggle to resolve these issues and may then be able to discuss them with the person in a gentle but truly beneficial manner.

Most authorities agree on the next phase as being one of "outward adjustment" (cf. Golan and Nadelson and Notman). Things seem to have gotten back to normal, and the victim may have returned to work or to normal domestic activities. She seems to be over the shock, as the defenses of rationalization, denial, and suppression take over. She may turn to close friends for support but is unlikely to discuss details of the occurrence.

The third stage is the classic one of "integration and resolution," in which the victim experiences a depressive reaction that may be stimulated by the need to reexamine the incident for legal reasons or because of conflicts over renewed sexual activity. The defenses do not work so well, and the person may experience fears about being alone, in crowds, or in any place that may be similar to the rape location. She often experiences nightmares or fantasies characterized by fear and violence. She may also begin to consider broader "women's issues," such as her job, her relationships with others, and her life-style in general.

It is important for crisis workers to remember that while these categories may be helpful for analysis, there will be a wide range of individual differences about the order, extent, or even the presence of these "stages." Just as one must employ Kübler-Ross' "stages" of death with a prudent sense that people may not seem to go through them at all, or may go through them at different rates or in mixed-up sequence, so the helper does not impose these stages of reaction on the rape victim. They do prepare the emergency worker to understand and respond to the *process of reaction* and to make sense of what might otherwise seem random and puzzling behavior. Such knowledge makes for timelier and more effective interventions.

SPECIAL PROBLEMS

It is also important for helpers to understand that the reaction to rape may vary according to the age and circumstances of the victim. There are special problems, for example, for young women, who are the principal victims of this crime. Not only can the experience color their attitudes toward men and sex, but it may, as Nadelson and Notman observe, bring up issues of separation and dependency. Parents and friends may offer support, but "they may also foster regression and prevent mastery of the stress and conflict evoked by the experience" (p. 27). The young victim may have trouble even allowing future medical examinations and may experience guilt in subsequent sexual relationships.

The divorced or separated woman has special problems because she may, cruelty compounded by cruelty, be thought of as somewhat responsible for the situation, as though it were "the kind of thing she might get herself into"; cultural attitudes toward the divorced or separated also subtly question their credibility, thus increasing the stress of the situation and making the support and understanding of the emergency worker all the more important. The likelihood of such persons perceiving the rape as a further defeat in life or as added evidence about their own personal inadequacy is higher than with other subjects.

Women with children, according to Nadelson and Notman (p. 27), have their problems compounded by the question of whether, how, and when to communicate to the children what has occurred. This is a very complicated situation because other members of the community may have knowledge of the incident and be the source of judgmental feedback to the family that can markedly affect the way the children view the mother. Problems with even the most supportive husbands frequently occur; the woman may well experience uncertainty about the way the husband now views her, and as the authors note, "since negative feelings toward a husband are not infrequent, she may become guilty or worried about these feelings and their implication for their future relationship."

Because the middle-aged woman may already be examining her life and its direction, the occurrence of rape may be particularly unsettling to her. Can she control her own life and can she manage on her own in a world that may be filled with threats and dangers? The consequences of rape are profound for all women but there is a special vulnerability to a woman at midlife; general reassurance is not enough at any stage.

A Longer View

What are the long-term effects of rape? Unfortunately, there is little reliable information about this. There are a number of issues that experienced clinicians have encountered (op. cit., p. 31), and these include:

1. A mistrust of men, resulting in problems or uncertainty in relationships.
2. Sexual problems of one kind or another.
3. Phobic reactions.
4. Anxiety and depression touched off by small cues that are remind-

ers of the original incident (e.g., music that was played that day, similar weather or activities).

5. Difficulty with future gynecological examinations, including anxiety and avoidance of them.

It is important for helpers to be aware of these possible problems, not in order to mention them unnecessarily or inappropriately but to sensitize themselves to picking up and understanding these signs when they appear some time after the rape experience. Helpers can then educate other family members or arrange for timely referrals for additional professional assistance.

What Can You Do?

Arbarbanel ("Helping Victims of Rape," *Social Work*) suggests the following as the areas of need for rape victims:

1. They need information about where to obtain legal, medical, and mental health services.

2. Immediate care for physical trauma, the gathering of medical-legal evidence, and the handling, treatment, or prevention of venereal disease and pregnancy.

3. Quick referral, after emergency help, for ongoing professional counseling.

4. Sensitive treatment from all who deal with them, including the police, medical assistants, lawyers, and even family members. The sensitive emergency worker may be able to mediate these encounters so that they are truly helpful.

5. Support from family and friends. This can also be orchestrated and mediated by the crisis worker who is aware of the mixed feelings or confusion that may be common among these psychologically significant persons.

Counselors pressed into service in the crisis of a rape should find out if any hospitals in the area have rape crisis centers. These are fairly common now, and the personnel there are prepared to handle most of the needs mentioned above. Seeking out this information before such emergencies arise is one of the most sensible things that crisis counselors can do because it enables them to make early and appropriate referral. It also gives them a sense of confidence about what they are doing. A calm and assured manner in a counselor may be an extremely important factor in helping the rape victim through the acute phase of the problem.

REPORTING THE RAPE

This is a complicated issue, but one that is sure to come up in the context of the emergency. Many victims simply do not wish to report the incident. This naturally lessens the possibility of any later successful prosecution, even though prosecution may provide an excellent outlet for the rage that victims feel. The process of prosecution, with all that it involves, is, however, also potentially traumatic for the victim, and this should be kept in mind. One should also remember that reporting is not something that should be insisted upon to satisfy the needs of other persons (e.g., either the outraged husband or a lawyer who has made a judgment about what is "best" for the person). No victim should be forced or even unduly pressured to report the rape to the authorities.

Helpers should be aware that means exist for reporting rapes anonymously. Some victims are willing to do this when they aren't willing to be more public about the rape. Reporting it, in whatever manner, may lessen their anxiety. In a larger sense, it may help in the education of the public and in the prevention of rape in the long-term.

SUMMING UP

Helpers should possess necessary practical information as well as the capacity and willingness to offer calm and understanding support to the victim. They should not push their own agenda or their own feelings, much less a schema or outline of stages of reaction. People differ, and they should be dealt with as they are, not as we suppose them to be.

Be ready for strong expressions of rage toward all men. The helper, if he is a man, may be the lightning rod for this. He should treat it as transference material and not take it personally.

It will be enormously beneficial if the crisis helper can make sure that another rational, supportive, "significant" person is present during the acute phase and for follow-up as well.

If the victim wishes to handle the details of the situation herself, allow her to do so. It will help her to regain a sense of control over both the situation and her life in general. However, the helper should watch for indications of overcontrol or intense suppression that reveal that the person is not quite as self-sufficient as she claims.

Helpers should not be surprised at the strong reactions on the part of husbands or other relatives and close friends. Dealing with the reactions of people may be one of the most helpful services that the emergency counselor can provide. The victim is not at all helped by the extreme anger or the desire for revenge that can sometimes develop in relatives or friends. These persons also need help to handle their own feelings maturely and to reach a calm, rational understanding of what the victim has experienced and of how they can constructively assist her.

For Further Reading

Arbarbanel, Gail, "Helping Victims of Rape." *Social Work* 6, (Nov. 1976), p. 478.

Boston Women's Health Collective. *Our Bodies, Ourselves*. New York: Simon and Schuster, 1976.

Golan, N. *Treatment in Crisis Situations*. New York: Free Press, 1978.

Groth, N. A., and Burgess, A. W. "Sexual Dysfunction During Rape." *New England Journal of Medicine* 297:14 (1977), p. 764.

Law Enforcement Assistance Administration. "Forcible Rape." *Sexuality Today,* August 1978.

Nadelson, Carol C., and Notman, Malkah T. "Emotional Repercussions of Rape." *Medical Aspects of Human Sexuality,* March 1977, p. 16.

Rada, Richard T. "Commonly Asked Questions about the Rapist." *Medical Aspects of Human Sexuality,* Jan. 1977, p. 52.

Thompson, K., and Medea, A. *Against Rape,* New York: Farrar, Straus and Giroux, 1974.

NINE

Loss and Mourning

WE all lose something every day. While not all these losses are major ones and so we don't feel the impact of most of them, they are remarkably similar to life's larger losses, both in their psychological structure and in the way they reproduce, on a miniature scale, the characteristics of these more serious events. One might become convinced, after some investigation of our human ways, that we are involved in the task of loss and gain all the time, that these are profoundly important to our sense of ourselves as well as to our sense of meaning, and that failing to attend to them can only penalize us and leave us less prepared to deal with major crises of loss when they do occur. We are rehearsing all the time, in other words, for letting go of persons, events, and what we might broadly describe as conditions of time (e.g., youth, the prime of life), while at the same time we are also processing or adjusting to what replaces each of these in our lives.

No counselor lacks experience, then, in the cycle of loss and renewal that is so central in the life of every human being. Our best preparation for being of assistance when others suffer loss is the fact that we ourselves are not strangers to it, that we have drunk its cup of bitterness, that we understand what the person is going through because we have made our own passage through the same difficulties. Helpers who attempt to be smooth and totally unruffled—those who feel that any betrayal of human reactions is a liability or a weakness—may make the strength of their own personalities less available to others at the very moment when this is the best thing they can offer them.

In other words, no matter how little professional training we may have had, we can still help persons who suffer the crisis of loss because we can understand, or at least recognize, this experience in our lives. Loss is one crisis to which we can respond if we have dealt psychologically and spiritually with our own losses. If we possess even a minimal capacity for empathy and the common sense to allow psychological processes to work themselves out without undue interference on our part, we can be of help to others at their time of loss.

IDENTIFYING LOSS

It is of course easy to identify major, and often tragic, losses: when a family member dies, or when a person's life is altered forever by illness or accident, for instance. So, too, we appreciate the sense of loss that goes along with divorce, separation, being fired from a job, or finding that a project to which one has devoted much energy and in which one has invested much hope is a failure.

It is more difficult to appreciate the experience of loss in a culture like ours, which to some extent at least has lost its sense of the tragic. And yet injury to and loss of self-esteem still occur regularly in every life. We may be handicapped in assaying their effects on us, however, because we have made losing at least a partial disgrace. Furthermore, we have discarded many of the rituals and symbols, especially in organized religion, that once enabled people to face and deal with the persistent appearance of loss in their lives.

The loss of youth, for example, results in a loss of dignity in the judgment of a culture that prizes it so much. The only thing people are allowed to lose respectably these days is weight. It has also become fashionable for people to lose their innocence and their ideals before they have understood the significance of either one or before they have learned to realistically modify their expectations of themselves and of life. Subtle losses abound, in other words, and the crisis that the counselor may be asked to deal with sometimes has its roots in a malaise of the spirit that is absolutely real yet extremely difficult to deal with in an era that doggedly refuses to face up to the inevitability of loss.

MANAGING OUR TROUBLES

The cultural difficulties are bad enough, but when we add to them some of the programs that have been developed to deal with human loss, then we can begin to understand the present complexity of facing straightforwardly the inexorable facts about loss and its place, along with grief and mourning, in our lives. Thus, for example, the overzealous desire to manage the process of dying by dividing it into phases that the counselor will oversee—and, perhaps, force us through, if need be—may be inherently sacrilegious, because it can defile or distort an experience that, in the end, persons must manage on their own.

So too, the cultural effort to familiarize people with death, to rob it of its mystery through naïve courses at, for example, the high school level, may only generate the deception that there is really nothing to lose when we die, that nothing strange or remarkable is going to happen to us. Dying in an orderly and knowing way is, however, as elusive as our search for a painless dentist, and counselors should be rightfully wary of those who, like the patent-medicine sellers of old, offer ways to outwit the pain of separation and loss that are linked so intimately with the true experience of being alive.

Counselors who have to deal with persons who have suffered loss must prepare themselves psychologically and philosophically for this work, and a key aspect of this is to be able to accept suffering as endemic to life. As a character in John Cheever's *The Wapshot Chronicle* learns, "There is no cure for Autumn, there is no medicine for the north wind."

The Shape of Grief

If a mature realism about the inevitability of loss is a fundamental attribute of the crisis counselor, specific and trustworthy information about grief and mourning is also essential. Perhaps the classic observations about these subjects were made by psychiatrist Erich Lindemann, who, as mentioned earlier, did pioneering work on mourning with the survivors and relatives of the victims of the Coconut Grove nightclub fire in Boston in 1942. Lindemann concluded that:

1. Acute grief is a definite syndrome that has psychological and physical symptoms.
2. This may appear immediately following the crisis of loss or it may be delayed until some time later on.
3. Distorted grief reactions may replace the typical syndrome. The symptoms may be exaggerated, only highlight one aspect of the loss, or may seemingly be absent altogether.
4. By the use of appropriate helping measures, distorted reactions may be transformed into normal grieving and the individual may be assisted to work out a successful solution of the crisis. ("Symptomatology and Management of Acute Grief," *American Journal of Psychiatry*).

Colin Parkes (*Bereavement: Studies of Grief in Adult Life*) has also done extensive work in charting the nature of grief's psychological arc, particularly in his follow-up investigations of bereaved spouses. Most people who do any counseling, even nonprofessionally, have become acquainted with Sigmund Freud's description of grief as work that we must do for ourselves before we can reemerge in life. Periods of mourning, once culturally approved, allowed persons the opportunity and recognized their need to do this work, much of which is symbolic and unconscious, but no less significant for that. Parkes explored this process and discovered some of the elements that, though we may not like to accept them, seem to be normal components of the grieving work of the bereaved.

He identified, for example, the existence of pangs of grief and the appearance of pining for the lost one, as well as a process of searching and yearning that may manifest itself in the sorrowing individual's life. Some of the elements of the search for the lost person may strike others as quite irrational, although when properly appreciated, these elements can be understood as profound efforts to make sense of or piece together the events of lives shattered by loss. Parkes also observed the feelings of guilt and anger that quickly arise in those who have lost a spouse through death, and how, later on, as these feelings diminish, they are replaced by experiences of apathy and depression.

The great contribution of Parkes is his integration of all these reactions as aspect of an overall process in which they are not only normal but also necessary for the accomplishment of grief work. It is particularly important for counselors to be aware of this larger process of mourning; otherwise, they may misinterpret individual actions or, through the best of their efforts, interfere with the natural working out of a fundamentally healthy human task.

The irrational search for the beloved, for example, is not so strange when it is understood as a natural and therefore unsurprising occurrence; it is symbolic, as many unconscious activities are, and does not readily fit into well-ordered categories. Family members who observe it may become excessively alarmed, believing that the activities associated with it are indications of something wrong with the grieving person. Understanding this behavior and interpreting it to family members can be reassuring and supportive to them. They in turn may best serve the grieving person by learning to tolerate some of these seemingly bizarre actions rather than trying to modify or stop them. Sometimes the grieving individual, who may be feeling many unanticipated reactions or may observe themselves engaging in what strikes them as irrational behavior, needs the same kind of reassurance that they are not going crazy.

In other words, a broad survey of the phenomena associated with mourning tells us again how wide the range of "normal" reactivity is.

Perhaps emergency counselors do some of their best work through the understanding and reassurance they can convey to persons who find themselves caught up in the whirlwind of a grief reaction. This is one of the areas where understanding and acceptance reveal their immense healing power. They do not constitute a cure, but they make it possible for the cure—the mourning process itself—to work.

In the long run, one way or the other and whether or not we recognize it for what it is, the mourning process has its way with all of us. Defenses against it never work completely, at least not for any length of time. Some helpers, such as teachers and preachers who are in a position to do so, may be able to assist people to deal with the crises of loss merely by speaking in public about its pervasive and normal character.

Just helping a person to identify what is occurring as something that is to be expected in the human condition provides enormous relief and support. It is especially helpful to show that death is not the only loss that demands mourning from us, and that we should anticipate grief reactions in other widely differing situations. These may include divorce, retirement, the departure of a favored child from home, or any other change in a relationship that is central in someone's life. The alleviation of a sense of having failed, or of guilt or shame over certain reactions, enormously helps persons to handle the crisis of loss.

UNDERSTANDING DEFENSES

The insertion of a counselor into a crisis of loss may require a prudent blend of activity and restraint. Mature counselors may well be able to trust their own instincts in these circumstances, but a few guideposts may serve at least as helpful reminders to all who find themselves in any way related to the emergency that is touched off by major loss.

First of all, psychological defenses demand our respect. Even when they are not of the highest order, defenses hold people together. They are the best people can manage to keep themselves in some kind of working order when the pressures are great, as they are, for example, when a loss takes place. Emergency helpers should not attack these defenses, trying, for instance, to provoke crying because they are sure it would be "good for the person." Nor should they attempt to apply, in cookbook fashion, to the lives of others any of the things they may have learned about such experiences as the stages of grief.

People go through the process of grief at their own rate and in their own way. Our task is to further this natural process, to make possible its occurrence even though this process may seem mysterious and trying to all who are in any way associated with it. Respect for the unconscious components of human personality demands that we exercise the greatest caution in any attempts to manipulate or rearrange the defensive patterns that we discover in persons during periods of grief.

Some skill in reading the defenses, in catching that pattern and being able to understand it as a part of a process, enables us to use our own human insights and strengths constructively during these crises. This sensitivity will lead us to allow people to hold on to their defenses, even when we would like to see them react in a different manner. If we allow people to do their grief work, supplying them with support and understanding, they will surrender their defenses in due time on their own. This will come from within, and it will in fact be a signal that they have completed their grief work and can reenter life once again in a full and healthy manner.

WHAT TO DO

Get used to grief. There is more than enough of it to go around, so do not make a crisis for yourself out of every grief situation that you must enter. Respect your own defenses just as you would the defenses of others. Listen to yourself and the messages you are giving and be sure that you understand these before you act. If, for example, you discover that you are overreacting, or if you want to avoid the crisis altogether because you have no taste for it, then you should try to work out the meaning of these feelings before you do anything to help others.

It need not take long, nor need it be very puzzling, to discover why we react as we do. Reasonably healthy people can trace their own emotional reactions in a few moments if they want to. What they discover is ordinarily not startling and is often familiar; it is part of the story of themselves that they have known about for some time.

Making a resolution that we will allow people the room and time to mourn demands that we do just that. It does not take much to convey to someone else that we are with them in their grief but that we are not going to intrude. Nor are we going to make excessive demands on them to behave differently. By the way we deal with the situation we can create a climate that helps everyone understand and deal with the event more sensitively and constructively. To that end we should make ourselves available to other family members and friends at the time of the crisis. They may well be able to take over, once we have assisted them in understanding some of the psychological aspects of the situation.

It is important in this regard to recognize that during the crisis of loss, *others*—the children or the in-laws of the dead person, the people who stand a step back from the principal mourner, the spouse—may need more attention than they usually get. They are going through their own grief work, and the occasion of the loss may tear loose adjustments that normally keep them together. Thus, for example, children who still have some residue of sibling rivalry may find that it surfaces during the stressful time of making funeral arrangements or when deciding on who will stay with or take care of the surviving spouse on a short- or long-term basis. These and any of a dozen other concerns and questions have the potential to cause emotional reactions that may be quite intense.

Counselors should not interfere here either, but they should be prepared to respond to these seemingly secondary aspects of the mourning situation. Such flare-ups are, of course, also normal; indeed, they are almost common, and in time they usually heal themselves. We should not be surprised by them or make people feel worse than they already do when these events occur.

Practical Helps

Some bereaved individuals need very concrete and practical assistance as well as the compassionate and wise emotional support that we have described. For example, a widow may need considerable support, and follow-up assistance as well, in sorting out the hundreds of details that must be dealt with after a husband dies. Sensible referrals for economic counseling and planning may be just as significant as anything else the emergency counselor does for the desolated individual. Some knowledge of community resources, through banks or lawyers, to assist in these matters should be part of every helper's expertise.

In episodes of loss the emergency counselor ordinarily has a role at the earliest stages of the experience. Some workers, however, such as members of the clergy, may contribute greatly by their follow-up interventions, which occur after the person is over the initial shock but when he or she is alone in facing the consequences of the loss. The commotion of the funeral, the visits of friends and family from far off are over with, and the long journey back to life lies before them.

The presence of a helper at this time, which is also a stage in the crisis, can be of major importance. This is a role that in many ways may be filled only by someone outside the family circle, someone with distance and perspective who can receive grief and its secrets without embarrassment and without provoking a sense of shame in the bereaved. Such counseling does not receive enough recognition for the significant role it can play in assisting the stricken person to work through the loss he or she has experienced. Follow-up work enables us both to continue offering practical help (about jobs, day-care, etc.) and to reassure the person about various experiences in the grief work that may otherwise seem very disturbing to them. It is not uncommon, for example, for persons to feel they have seen the lost person in brief and fleeting glimpses. This can be very distressing unless the counselor offers reassurance on this matter.

This may also be the time to help the person join a group, such as those for widows, that are active in many cities, for the support that may be received through contact with others who have gone through the same experiences.

A TIME TO REFER

It may only be at this later date that the true nature of the crisis becomes obvious to the helper, when it may be seen that the mourning is distorted to a pathological extent. Thus, when there seems to be no grief at all, or when the bereaved's insistence that all is well just doesn't ring true, or when the bereaved begins to complain of the same illness that the lost spouse suffered from, a counselor should carefully evaluate whether the person should seek ongoing professional psychological assistance. Nonprofessionals should not in any way attempt to deal with such situations in a psychological manner. A gentle but purposeful referral can make a great difference in how the suffering person eventually resolves this crisis in mourning.

For Further Reading

Bowlby, John. "Process of Mourning," *International Journal of Psychoanalysis* 42 (1961), p. 317.

Freud, Sigmund. "Mourning and Melancholia." In *Collected Papers*, vol. IV. London: Hogarth Press, 1950.

Gorer, G. *Death, Grief and Mourning in Contemporary Britain*. London: Cresset, 1965.

Hersey, Jean. *A Widow's Pilgrimage*. New York: Continuum Books, 1979.

Lindemann, Erich, "Symptomatology and Management of Acute Grief." *American Journal of Psychiatry* 101 (1944), p. 141.

Parkes, Colin M., M.D. *Bereavement: Studies of Grief in Adult Life*. New York: International Universities Press, 1972.

TEN

Drug Abuse: What Is It?

IT is easier to define drug abuse than it is to get anyone, even in the midst of a full-blown crisis, to admit that this is the problem for him or her. In general, it can be defined as the excessive or indiscriminate use of any drug, including prescription drugs, over-the-counter remedies, and all others. Alcohol, caffeine (in coffee, diet pills, cola drinks, etc.) and tobacco are all drugs which can be abused.

Common sense helps us to distinguish use from abuse. Obviously, many persons use drugs occasionally without incurring physical or psychological harm. Unfortunately, the persons in drug-related emergencies may also claim that such temperate use characterizes their lives. Even the least experienced counselor should be ready for this, and be able to make independent judgments about the signs that go along with a genuine drug problem.

Drug abusers are those who use drugs so often, or in such inappropriate situations, that significant alterations occur in their life-style. These changes affect a broad range of phenomena, including physical health, personality development, social relations, self-perception, the carrying out of necessary every-day responsibilities, and financial well-being. How does one make a judgment? A simple rule of thumb for nonprofessionals is this: A drug abuse problem exists if the person's life would be qualitatively better without the use of the drugs involved. If we hope to be helpful, we must become crisis-sensitive in this regard and ask this question early, and without false embarrassment.

WHY IS IT COMPLICATED?

Drug abuse can be a smoldering crisis, one that is truly insidious, because a serious drug habit can be maintained only by a vast array of interpersonal and intrapersonal reinforcements. Virtually any psychological state can be altered in any direction that is desired through the use of legal or illegal drugs. People generally begin their use of drugs in early adolescence, largely because they have heard about their effects and wish to experiment, an all too human inclination. A deeper motivation may be the simple desire to take a substance that perceptibly changes the way one feels, both physically and psychologically.

It is a mistake, in other words, to presume that drug-taking is born in adolescent rebellion or that it is a sign of it. Drug use is born in the cultural-medical context of our society and may be related more to curiosity than rebellion. Individuals begin to learn about drugs the first time they experience a pleasurable change in themselves as a result of something external's being used either in or on their bodies.

One should anticipate drug abuse as a natural consequence of social conditions that both accept and approve the use of chemical substances to relieve unpleasantness. Drugs are, after all, widely used to relieve pain, anxiety, boredom, fatigue, excitement, and frustration. Drug usage is powerfully reinforced by the commonly reported subjective feelings of users that they experience increased, if not superior, social facility. If drug use is coupled with the perception of desirable consequences, it is not surprising that the drug is used again. This holds true even when other, undesirable consequences also follow. Hangovers and withdrawal symptoms are not punishing enough to break the bond between use and reward that is a sign of a developing drug-abuse crises.

Drug abuse is a serious problem for young people precisely because their sense of identity—their ego—is still in a formative stage. They are always on the lookout for some behavior or activity that will make them feel that they are masters of their personal and social worlds. Drug use seems like the short-cut to such self-confidence; if it seems to work in delivering popularity and self-esteem, the drug becomes a key to life that is hard to relinquish. Some adults may use drugs for the same reason, but the dangers are more obvious for the young, who are struggling to achieve a sense of themselves and their own adequacy. Peer pressure is also an enormous factor in creating a drug-crisis climate because it plays on the desperate need of the young to be approved in their own social milieu. The young are also quick to attribute their popularity or social ease to the drug rather than to any reliable internal sense of social adequacy. The very absence of a well-defined sense of self makes them vulnerable to the use of artificial props.

THE SUBTLE CRISIS

Drug abuse in a highly dramatic form is not often encountered in what we might term a "pure state." The crisis is often masked by other life crises, such as financial, educational, medical, or marital problems. These are the obvious crises that flower up, like an atomic cloud, from the explosive use of drugs. So much time and money are consumed in abusing drugs that the normal functioning of the individual becomes severely taxed and breakdowns occur in areas such as those mentioned above. The increased stress of such problems merely intensifies the temptation to use drugs as an escape or an illusory solution. And cruelly enough, drug use may temporarily relieve stress, thus reinforcing itself and compounding the problem, which gradually becomes a vast netted mass of emotional need.

Alcoholism is still the drug-abuse problem par excellence; it is the most pervasive and exacts the highest social and economic costs from those affected even indirectly by it. However, alcoholism's dubious status is currently being challenged by the rapid increase in the use of prescription drugs. These include three major types: (1) barbiturates and sedatives, (2) stimulants such as diet pills, and (3) tranquilizers such as Librium and Valium. These drugs are not as difficult to secure as one might suppose since they are at times prescribed freely by general physicians, who view them as specific aids for patient complaints. Many persons have learned the code, that is, the type of complaint that will get them the prescription drug they desire. It is also true that some disreputable professionals have made drugs illicitly available. Estimates of how extensive this crisis is are generally inaccurate because no records exist that would reflect the number of pills prescribed or sold, or for what purposes, during any given time period. Drug companies, not surprisingly, keep a low profile in regard to such matters.

DIRECT CRISES

Some crises that center explicitly on the abuse of drugs do exist. An example is the accidental or intentional overdose, an emergency that is documented almost every day in the newspapers. Some abusers also suffer severe medical problems when they mix drugs of different types. For example, an abuser may take one drug and then a different one in order to counteract the effects of the first one, as is the case with an individual who takes a sedative to relax or sleep and then a stimulant in order to wake up.

When a nonprofessional helper becomes involved in an overdose situation, it is clear that immediate medical treatment is needed. The best initial service he or she can provide is to see that this is made available. The nonprofessional may also help by finding out what drugs have been taken and in what quantity. This can then be communicated to the medical doctor, who will need this information in order to render emergency treatment.

We won't burden those who wish to be helpful in this situation with a long list of "Don'ts"; we will just give one blanket recommendation: "Don't do anything else." Time is wasted by those who feel that they can somehow provide first aid through pouring coffee into the drugged person or walking them in the fresh air. Our best service in this drug-abuse emergency is first to get responsible medical assistance as swiftly as possible and then to keep bystanders out of the way.

DISCOVERING DRUGS AT HOME

A direct crisis may also occur when parents find drugs in the possession of their children. Obviously, this can quickly become a highly emotional scene, marked by overreactions on the part of both adults and children. But such possession is hardly ever an "end of the world" phenomenon, and helpers may offer great assistance merely by working to get the situation into proper perspective. Many parents resort too swiftly to extreme methods, such as calling juvenile authorities or the police, in hopes that such actions will scare the young back into good behavior. Bringing these people into this problem may at times be necessary, but they should be the last rather than the first steps taken in any of these incidents. A criminal or psychiatric record can be just as damaging to many young people as the drugs themselves.

Counselors can help those involved to handle the emotional frustration that accompanies such occurrences and should aim at facilitating frank, objective, and nonmoralistic exchanges between the parents and the youngster. It can be particularly useful for the concerned parties to exchange information instead of judgmental statements or defensive explanations. Frequently the child knows more about drugs than the parents do, both in the "street" sense and in regard to known medical findings.

Mothers and fathers can only profit from learning accurate information about drugs before they take action one way or another. One of the most constructive services that nonprofessional counselors can provide is access to this information, either through their own efforts or through referrals. They can also help the parents air their emotional conflicts about the situation so that they can then learn something of the facts before they take action. When elders act harshly or before they have educated themselves about the nature of drugs involved, younger people often feel more isolated and tend to persist in taking the drugs in a more secretive way.

WHAT TO LOOK FOR

Counselors are not necessarily diagnosticians, but, using prudent reserve, they may be able to detect the symptoms of a looming drug crisis. Thus they may be able either to intervene constructively or to provide outside help at a time when it can really do some good. Helpers should therefore understand some of the behaviors and reactions that accompany drug abuse. This is a variegated and confusing picture, however, because such drugs often have different effects on different subjects, depending on a number of factors, including drug potency, body metabolism, psychological expectations, environment (setting), and the extent to which the drug is taken in combination with other substances.

Another enormously important variable centers on the fact that users have no guarantee that they *have* taken what they *think* they have taken. An incredible number of white crystalline powders exist, along with an incredible number of drug names, and the combinations can be infinitely complex.

Counselors should be on the outlook for the most general kinds of symptoms, the most reliable of which is *change.* Any noticeable change in the activity level of the individual, whether increased or decreased, should be noted. Similarly, any change in physical appearance through weight loss or gain should not be ignored. So, too, any shift in patterns of sleeping or waking as well as changes in motivation and affect—from manic exuberance to uncaring indifference—are important signals.

Helpers are only using common sense when they note the potential significance of a change in the subject's social environment, that is, a shift to a different crowd of friends or associates. Another symptom that counselors should read carefully in conjunction with these is increased furtiveness, or, as some have called it, "nonclinical paranoia," especially in regard to authorities such as school principals or teachers, the police, or others who occupy similar positions in culture.

There is no substitute for good judgment in identifying or acting upon the presence of these symptoms in an individual. Restraint is almost always in order. Counselors who attempt to seek further information about an individual for whom they are concerned should also remember that, characteristically, drug abusers have a vested interest in distorting the true facts and circumstances of their abuse problem. Their first allegiance is not to the helper but to their drug; even when they claim that they want help, they care more about their drug than they do about somebody trying to find out about their lives. Tact and a capacity for patient understanding are essential for those who wish to be constructive in a potential or actual drug crisis.

WHEN IT CAN HAPPEN

In *The Drug Dilemma,* Sidney Cohen lists twelve situations in which susceptible individuals may abuse drugs. Counselors should be sensitive to these possibilities:

1. Severely inadequate, immature, depressed, psychotic, or borderline personalities, who seek a quick and magical solution for their character defects.

2. Curious people with the opportunity and the money to afford drugs.

3. "Joy-riders" or people who feel bored with their everyday lives.

4. Compliant persons with a strong need to belong to a group who come under strong social or peer pressure.

5. Artists who seek to refuel their inspiration.

6. People with a real or imagined need to escape a certain situation.

7. Accidental addicts who become hooked at an age or in circumstances in which they are unable to discriminate or to object.

8. Those strongly persuaded by a "significant other," such as a lover or a family member.

9. People suffering real stress from overwork or other negative life circumstances.

10. Impulsive and poorly controlled people who "try anything" because they have little realistic regard for their lives.

11. Those who have had a previous history of abuse and who seem to have quit.

12. Those seeking personal insights or some variety of religious experience.

ADDICTIVE PERSONALITY?

It is hard to specify the existence of this personality type, although one will find this term still in use. Many experts do not believe that there is a clear-cut addictive personality. They do discuss the "inadequate" personality as the broad general category in which abusers may be found. People whose personalities are not yet well-formed, such as young adolescents, can, therefore, be markedly susceptible to drug abuse.

In short- or long-term treatment, emphasis is frequently placed on understanding the contingencies that support the abuse and devising a plan to alter the life-style of the abuser in order to provide experiences that reinforce behaviors that depend upon abstinence. This may require the application of resources from many spheres, including the family, school, work, and religious and moral supports.

ADVICE FOR NONPROFESSIONALS

Become informed about the current drug-abuse patterns that are likely to appear in the population with whom you most frequently work. Don't try to become an expert; a working knowledge will do just fine.

Slang terms come and go very swiftly. In speaking with someone caught up in a drug crisis, try to use the language that he or she uses. That may require a regular revision of one's knowledge of slang, so it is important to also try to find out the common trade name of the drug involved. The *Physician's Desk Reference* is a valuable source of information about side effects.

Don't play district attorney or Grand Inquisitor. If the abuser perceives us as passing judgment or gathering evidence, he or she will probably distort the truth in order to defend the drug habit.

Be ready to make a referral and do not be disappointed if this is the only action you can take when summoned into the middle of a full-blown emergency. Efforts to coerce people into treatment are hardly ever successful. Sometimes we must leave the drug abuser alone with the information about medical or other therapeutic help, knowing that they may not act immediately on our recommendation. People who have built their adjustment around drugs are not about to surrender this habit or modify it quickly.

Be modest in your expectations of yourself. While nonprofessionals can offer a certain amount of solid assistance, they cannot do everything. If you don't demand of yourself that you be a savior, you may free yourself to give, with greater effectiveness, the help that you do have to offer.

Know what you are talking about and don't speak in presumptions or half-truths. Drug abusers are unusually sensitive in this regard, and if you give evidence of being poorly informed, they will write you off and at the same time justify themselves.

For Further Reading

Bennett, J. C., and Demos, G. D. *Drug Abuse and What We Can Do About It*. Springfield, Ill.: Charles C. Thomas, 1970.

Blum, R. H. *Students and Drugs*. San Francisco: Jossey Bass, 1969.

Bockar, J. A. *Primer for the Non-Medical Psychotherapist*. New York: Halsted Press, 1976.

Cohen, S. *The Drug Dilemma*. New York: McGraw-Hill, 1969.

ELEVEN

Problems of Relationships

A playwright once described the creation of the world as "a long slow miracle." So too, in the miracle of pregnancy and birth there may not only be wondrous moments and periods of self-realization and growth but a long, slow crisis as well. The crisis may not be a singular event but an intricate pattern of the unpredictable and the unspoken, the true nature and destructive power of which may not become evident for years.

It is possible, for example, that some of the seemingly well-adjusted couples who abruptly hire a lawyer and head for the divorce court after the last child has left home may have been estranged for a long period of time, in a state of crisis that resembled a time-release medication. Such problems often go back to the period of pregnancy and childbirth. These momentous events can cause great stress and generate serious misunderstandings between the husband and wife who are thrown out of synchronization by the challenges of becoming a father and mother.

Members of the clergy and physicians, especially, among nonprofessional counselors, may be involved in these situations on an almost daily basis since they are the ones who most often have contact with couples, both before and after their marriages, at most of the significant events in their lives. It is to them, in general, that the married couple turns, singly or together, for both sound information and helpful counsel. Unfortunately, nonprofessionals such as these frequently do not understand the significance of their potential role during the time of pregnancy. They often fail to give more than general reassurances, when they could, fairly simply, provide support and factual explanations that could help the couple get through this the difficult time of adjustment without the experience's turning into a crisis.

CHANGING A RELATIONSHIP

Having a child necessarily and permanently alters the manner in which husband and wife relate to each other. A failure to appreciate this or the kinds of constantly shifting adjustments that this demands will almost certainly lead to a crisis. Indeed, having a child is an event strewn with combustible psychological materials looking for a sparklike precipitant. What are some of the issues that mark the course of pregnancy?

Psychiatrists Paul Brenner and Martin Greenberg ("The Impact of Pregnancy on Marriage," *Medical Aspects of Human Sexuality*) have provided a helpful review of the most important issues. They cite the truth—as much a part of human wisdom as it is of medical lore—that despite a couple's initial positive reaction to pregnancy, a change in the marital relationship has already begun. Something profound has occurred to both man and woman, who, now on the verge of becoming parents, must put their childhood behind. They are involved, at many levels of their personalities, in making a generational passage, and this in itself is a critical time for them. Not even living together for an extended period of time beforehand really prepares a young couple for the challenge of change that goes with married life. It is also obvious that if the couple already have unresolved differences, adding a new member to the household is hardly a solution, although it may serve as an enormous distraction. Even for a couple truly devoted to each other, the strain of reshaping their stance toward each other is severe, and the assistance of understanding helpers may prove crucial to their accomplishing this successfully.

SPECIFIC ASPECTS

As Greenberg and Brenner point out, women are often disturbed and perplexed at their own reactions during the first months of being pregnant. They are emotionally elated and yet they suffer morning sickness and fatigue; they feel out of joint with themselves and may possibly feel confused or guilty.

Man and woman may experience different reactions to sexual relationships during the period of pregnancy. Generalizations are next to impossible in this area, but only the naïve could imagine that the adjustment here would be made without difficulty. Men and women can get out of phase with each other, and, especially if they are not helped to share their feelings intelligently and sensitively, they may experience an estrangement that could have long-lasting effects. Masters and Johnson have found, for example, that some men have their first affair during their wife's pregnancy, because at this particular time they often feel left out, deprived, or do not know how to express or explore their problems with their wives.

Husbands frequently fear that having sexual relations will cause some harm to the unborn infant. A hundred old folktales haunt the couple as they seek to adjust themselves to this new state of affairs. They may begin to experience what for them are unwelcome fantasies about themselves or about their own mothers, and these are upsetting and alienating for them.

One must also recognize that some medical condition may actually exist that dictates a certain restraint and caution in sexual relationships during pregnancy. Physicians bear a special responsibility to deal with each couple on an individual basis and to make their counsel fit the particular situation. Unfortunately, some physicians give highly restrictive general advice in the same way to everyone. This may heighten the stress of the man and woman, who need not only advice but also a chance to express their own questions and doubts. The role of the helper in providing understanding that furthers communication between husband and wife is essential when these matters are brought up.

In the last three months of pregnancy the woman may experience herself in a new and positive way because of the bodily changes, such as engorgement of the breasts, that she undergoes. As her term draws near, however, she may feel differently, experiencing herself as awkward and hoping that she will soon be delivered.

While the woman is becoming more profoundly involved, the man may feel progressively more left out. He cannot, much as he might try, completely share her feelings. It is not unknown for men to experience psychosomatic complaints at this critical time. Toothaches and upset stomachs and other similar complaints sketch poignantly the stress that the man feels as the changes of the childbearing time are worked out.

Observers have also reported that some men feel progressively detached and at an unconcerned distance from what is taking place. Brenner and Greenberg report that some of the wives they interviewed said that their spouses simply "disappeared" at this time. Once again, a sensitive counselor could identify the symbolic meaning of such behavior and help both husband and wife to realize its significance. Other indications that the husband is displacing his energies may be observed in the time and effort he may devote to sports, business, or research, all of which may be dropped once the child is born.

WHAT CAN COUNSELORS DO?

It may seem unsporting to point out that no counselor carries magic in his or her bag. There is something infinitely better than that, however, and that is old-fashioned understanding, seasoned, if you will, with common sense. If counselors do help the couple to talk to each other during what we have termed the long, slow crisis of pregnancy, they will contribute enormously to the happiness and good adjustment of the new family.

It does not require profound skill to catch the significance of what motivates the behavior that we have described; it does demand some investment of the self, a willingness to push beyond the genial good wishes and bland concern that some clergy and doctors supply during the time of pregnancy. Because it is such an enormously sensitive period in a couple's life together, any assistance that enables them to understand what is happening to them is both comforting and supportive and diminishes the intensity of this frequently unclassified crisis.

The counselor's chief way of intervening in this crisis is by speaking aloud the words that lie, half-formed at best, in the hearts of the couple. Just verbalizing fears and questions lifts away their power over others. It may be sensible to help young couples anticipate the difficulties that can occur, thereby educating them and preparing them emotionally to deal constructively with themselves and their relationship when critical incidents actually do occur.

AFTER THE CHILD IS BORN

Human reactivity is broad and varied, and some women may experience a sense of loss, just as they would if some limb had been surgically removed. They find that they are different, and they are puzzled that they should feel low after feeling so exalted at the time of birth. The husband, who may feel very pleased with his masculine achievement in fathering a child, may find himself absorbed totally in the child's existence and condition. Both parents have been through a dramatic event and they need the understanding presence of a counselor, almost always a nonprofessional, who knows how to "talk them down" gently as they turn to the new routine of family life.

"Presence" is the special quality of the helper whose main work is in some other profession. Just as the main value of the husband in the classes preparatory to childbirth is his presence with his wife, so too the pastor or the doctor, listening carefully but not intruding, can make a significant difference in the management of setting up family life. They may not have to provide specific information, although, naturally, they should do this as well as they can, but they do have to provide the simplest home-blessing of all, understanding.

There may be misgivings and regrets after the child is born. There may be an unforeseen physical problem. There will be reactions to each of these, but even those without much psychological training can help others work them through quite successfully.

AFTER THE CHILD IS HOME

The possibilities of critical events occurring at home are almost endless, particularly if it is the first child because everything is new for the couple. Even previously sound relationships will find themselves under psychological siege as husband and wife, now father and mother, find their way as best they can in their new roles.

It is not uncommon for the father, who may previously have felt somewhat on the outside of things, to become, as mentioned before, thoroughly engrossed in the new child, and, as a consequence, to neglect to pay enough attention to his wife, who may need extra concern and sensitivity as she adjusts to being a mother at home. Although there has been considerable modification of traditional family arrangements in the United States, the main care of the new baby is still the mother's responsibility; she does not have the opportunities for distraction, stimulation or esteem that daily work provides for the husband.

To avoid unnecessary crises, it may be helpful for counselors to focus on the communication that is essential for a continued good relationship between the spouses. There need be nothing romantic about this; the important issue centers on their telling each other what they really feel and not allowing misunderstandings to build up or to become impacted, so that they permanently alter the couple's attitudes toward each other. Misunderstandings here are the fuel for the crisis that may not find its precipitant until months or years later.

The relationship must change, and so the helper should acknowledge the distortion that a new child introduces into a formerly unquestioned marriage, helping the man and woman to recognize this and to live with it, so that they can continue to live successfully with each other. If the father feels jealous—a not uncommon reaction—because of the attention the baby is getting from the mother, he may feel guilty and uncomfortable. If he has no help in understanding what is happening to him, he may dangerously and destructively misinterpret his wife's attitude.

The life-style of the couple will inevitably be transformed, and a close couple may be surprised at what happens to them when they find that they must now share their attention and affection. They may not be accustomed to that and may discover the surrender of freedom is a greater challenge than they had anticipated.

The babies themselves are striking sources of stimulation, depending on the relative charm, healthiness, and responsivity of their personalities. The child is uniquely himself or herself, and parents who expected someone different need to adjust to that, even as they are getting used to a new and quite different daily routine.

There can be a definite crisis if the child does not measure up to parental expectations in some way or other. So, too, a crisis may arise when the child is suddenly perceived as an overwhelming responsibility.

SEXUAL RELATIONS

There is still more bad advice than good on the subject of sexual relationships during and after pregnancy. The best thing counselors can do is to acknowledge that they have very little expertise in this area and that they should refrain from handing on suggestions that may prove to be insensitive, wrong and additional fuel for the flare-up of crisis. Physicians have often used an arbitrary six-week figure as the time to wait before resuming normal sexual intercourse. Once again no such recommendation should be made without some discussion with the partners that involves them as responsible agents of decision. Reactions vary greatly in both men and women, and in the long run, it is a highly personal matter in which no outsider should interfere.

On the other hand, some knowledge of the medical and psychological aspects of this issue is also indispensable to any helper. This enables the pastor or doctor to facilitate the couple's dealing with the task of developing a new pattern of sexual intimacy, one that must now establish itself in relationship to a new human being, who will make claims on and transform the nature of the couple's closeness. One of the critical elements in the transition to family life is the loss of the intimacy that was once so easily available, when there was nobody else to consider.

The field of sexual intimacy will also be affected by the changes, physical and psychological, that have taken place, especially in the woman. There is no telling what the reaction of either party will be; what *is* certain is that some adjustment, some new learning, some demand on love and understanding will definitely occur.

One commonly reported reaction of women during pregnancy is a desire for physical closeness but not necessarily for sexual relationships. Many women report that they wish to be held closely by their husbands. This may be true in other circumstances as well, but it is surely important for counselors to assist husbands to understand this reaction and to encourage them to offer the special support that such holding seems to provide. Counselors need not be overly curious to be able to provide some helpful information or references if doubts or questions are presented to them. Their main role, however, remains that of providing the understanding that enables man and woman to speak to and hear each other during the prolonged, surprising, and sometimes unnerving period of adjustment that extends throughout pregnancy and into the months of settling in as a family. This is real crisis intervention. It is not as clearly dramatic as that which takes place after a major trauma, but in its long-range consequences it is among the best of the many good works that nonprofessional counselors do.

Perhaps one could classify all of marriage as a long, slow crisis. It behooves counselors to appreciate the truth that couples do not sail away into a twilight of bliss and that a counselor's interventions, when they are timed right, can be extremely helpful to a growing family. Additional children generate pressures in a different way, as, indeed, do all issues concerning their growth and development. Sensitivity to the strains thereby placed on the married couple is a great help at all of these points.

For Further Reading

Brazelton, T. B. *Infants And Mothers: Differences in Development.* New York: Delacorte Press, 1969.

Brenner, P., and Greenberg, M. "The Impact of Pregnancy on Marriage," *Medical Aspects of Human Sexuality* (July 1977), pp. 14–24.

Greenberg, M., and Morris, N. "Engrossment: The Newborn's Impact on the Father," *American Journal of Orthopsychiatry* 44:4 (1974) p. 520.

Masters, W. H., and Johnson, V. E. *Human Sexual Response.* Boston: Little, Brown, 1968.

Meyerowitz, J. H., and Fedlman, H. *Transition to Parenthood.* Psychiatric Research Report 20 (Feb. 1966), American Psychiatric Association.

Rogawski, A. "How Children Affect the Marital Sexual Relationship," *Medical Aspects of Human Sexuality* (June 1976).

TWELVE

A Child Has Been Abused

AMERICANS have grown acutely aware of the problem of battered and otherwise abused children over the past several years. A subject that was once not talked about openly, that was inconsistently and vaguely reported and not identified as a syndromelike phenomenon with distinctive patterns, child abuse has finally been dramatized as a real and present, if not entirely new, problem. Its presence constitutes a many-sided crisis, and nonprofessional counselors, from clergy to lawyers, are frequently the first to hear about its occurrence. Understanding the nature of this almost repugnant problem is essential if timely and sensible assistance is to be provided.

WHAT IS CHILD ABUSE?

Child abuse, according to Fontana and Besharove in *The Maltreated Child* (p. 91), takes place when a parent or other person either harms or threatens to harm the physical or emotional health of a child. Harm can occur when physical or mental injury is inflicted on the child, including injuries sustained as a result of excessive corporal punishment, or when an adult fails to supply the child with adequate food, clothing, shelter, education, or health care. It can also come when the adult abandons the child or commits some sexual offense against the child.

Obviously, child abuse may be understood either as an act of commission or omission. While it is true that some authorities make a distinction between the concepts of "abuse" and "neglect," it is difficult to say which is worse or whether they are essentially different, because both expose the child to potentially serious harm.

92

How Big a Problem?

Child abuse is an ugly and unpleasant fact of life, and although it may fall into the category of problems we would rather not have to face, its measured incidence suggests that in our culture any helper may have to deal with it, in critical form, on almost any day. Several authorities suggest that child abuse is the single most common cause of death in children. It is also a problem that seems to be spread across all racial groups in fairly equal fashion.

Statistics concerning child abuse are subject to all the problems that are associated with bringing a socially undesirable act to public attention. As a result the number of reported cases is presumed to represent only a fraction of the number of cases that actually exist.

In 1978 Kempe and Kempe wrote in *Child Abuse* that such abuse occurs, that is, is actually reported, 320 times per million population. This estimate suggests a yearly total of 115,000 children. Other researchers have come up with different figures. One government source claims that 60,000 children are "abused" every year. Dr. Vincent De-Francis suggests that 30,000 to 40,000 children are "battered" every year, 100,000 children are sexually abused every year, and 200,000 to 300,000 are psychologically abused during that time period.

Others contend that actual incidence of abuse may be ten times higher than the reported incidence, although media attention and new legislation have greatly increased the number of cases that are brought to light. In Illinois, in the fiscal year ending June 30, 1979, 24,807 cases of child abuse were reported. That was an 84 percent increase in the number of cases reported over the figures for the previous year. Public awareness of the critical nature of the problem has substantially increased, as has our willingness to face and deal with this evidence of the underside of human nature.

What Is the Abuser Like?

No completely satisfactory profile of the child abuser has as yet been drawn up. The literature on the subject has, however, yielded a number of factors that abusers seem to have in common.

For example, there is frequently a background of severe childhood deprivation; many of those who as adults abuse children were themselves abused in childhood.

The child who is the victim is viewed by the punishing parents as unfavorable or in some way disappointing.

The one who abuses is often socially isolated and has nobody to turn to when the tension of the rising crisis begins.

Poverty, alcoholism, illegitimacy, unwanted pregnancy and drug abuse are factors that notably increase the risk of child abuse. These factors are not, however, as significant as the following psychological patterns:

Adults whose dependency needs were not met as children and who had parents with very high expectations who doled out affection to them in a conditional and selective manner frequently find and choose mates with very similar backgrounds. When they give birth to children, they tend to view them immaturely, that is, as a source of gratification for themselves. When such parents fail to meet each other's emotional needs, something that frequently occurs, because of the depth of their needs and their own undeveloped psychological states, the "abuser personality" turns to the child instead. If the child cannot meet his or her needs—and most, of course, cannot (to ask a child to do so is a form of abuse in itself)—the parent's frustration builds to the flash point and the anger is taken out on the child.

Imbedded in this brief characterization of the abuser are several discernible psychological features. These include a low tolerance for frustration, poor impulse control, and a lack of trust in others. One might also observe a high sensitivity to criticism and a sense of blinding righteousness about discipline, especially the use of corporal punishment. Abusers also tend to identify the child with the less healthy aspects of their own personality, saying such things as, "The kid was born to raise hell, just like me," to similar sentiments, however crudely worded. Furthermore, these persons generally have a poor sense of themselves and low self-esteem, as well as inappropriate expectations of children, on whom they may psychologically feed, draining a child's spirit more truly than Dracula ever drew blood from his victims.

WHEN DOES THE EXPLOSION OCCUR?

The actual incident of harming the child occurs after a coalescence of life stresses becomes too much for the immature personality to manage any further. The explosion of anger often takes place when the person has, in his or her perception, suffered the last bearable problem or assault by life. The immediate stimulus, or precipitant, is ordinarily something that is developmentally normal for the child, such as crying, soiling clothes, or even failing to be as responsible or "charming" as the parents would like, or need the child to be, at the moment.

Helpers may easily identify what we might term a "cycle" of child abuse, which begins with the unmet parental needs that in turn generate expectations that the child can and, in fact, should meet these needs. At this point, some life crisis increases the parent's needs; when the child cannot meet these needs, the sequelae of frustration, abuse, and subsequent guilt then adds to the parental load of stress and can set off the cycle once more. This vicious circle of parent-child interaction may continue as a sickening kind of life-style unless some intervention takes place. The presence of such a cycle constitutes a crisis in which the helper must be prepared to act quickly and sensibly.

When abuse is a feature of a family with both parents present, one is usually the active abuser while the other subtly encourages or condones the abuse and helps to cover it up. It has been speculated that more abuse may occur in two-parent families because a spouse who reinforces the behavior is more dangerous than no spouse at all.

DISTRESS FLAGS

Helpers must be able to read and accurately identify the signals that portend a rapidly developing critical point. There is of course no substitute for good clinical judgment in integrating these signs into a pattern that demands intervention. There are, however, clear and concrete behaviors that can serve as the basis for that judgment. Observing and acting on them constitute the best steps in the prevention of child abuse.

These include situations and signs such as the following:

- A pregnancy during which the woman complains about the burden while at the same time voicing excessive expectations for the baby.
- Birth of a defective or abnormal child to parents such as those previously described.
- Illness or some other family trauma (death of close relative, etc.) during the pregnancy or after the birth of the child.
- Unexplained minor injuries to the child.
- Parents giving vague or diffuse accounts of a child's sickness or injury.
- Parents or parent appearing frequently at successive hospitals and clinics.

SIGNALS IN THE CHILDREN

The observant helper is aided in forming a judgment about the need for intervention when the ingredients for a battering crisis are present: a potentially abusing father or mother, a child, and some sudden increase in stress through a critical problem. Clues about the abuse or the battering may also be identified if any of certain characteristic reactions are present in the children. Fontana and Bersharov (*The Maltreated Child*) list, among others, the following (p. 28ff):

· If the child seems unduly afraid of his or her parents or unusually fearful in general. It is even more clear if the child is kept confined in one way or another for excessive periods of time. One might observe evidence of repeated skin abrasion or other injuries; these injuries are not treated sensibly in terms of bandages or medication.
· If the child appears undernourished or if the parents feed the child inappropriate food, drink, or medicine. The same holds true if the child is not dressed correctly for the prevailing weather conditions.
· If the child cries excessively or is described by the parents in some negative fashion, such as "bad" or "different," or, in fact, behaves in a way to live up to these labels.
· One can detect trouble if the child seems to have to take the parental role, attempting to protect or otherwise care for the parents' needs.
· A problem of battering or abuse may explain a child who is notably aggressive or destructive of property or, on the other hand, passive and withdrawn.

Physicians should be particularly alert to certain facts that may be elicited during the taking of a history at the time of a medical examination. Doctors should know, for example, that most child abuse takes place with children under three years of age; they should observe any signs that the child's general health has been neglected and carefully find out the history associated with any injuries or fractures the child may have sustained. It is helpful to find out if the child has been previously treated for any problems that may be observed, and if there has been a history of similar episodes, or if there have been many visits to different doctors or emergency rooms for treatment.

WHAT CAN THE EMERGENCY COUNSELOR DO?

One of the most difficult and yet essential things for us to do when we observe a critical situation of child abuse or battering is to inspect our own feelings to make sure that we have them under control. Few situations rouse as much anger as the beating of an innocent child. We cannot assume the role of vigilantes or those who seek revenge, or we will intervene in a destructive manner that may make things worse then they already are. Nonetheless, the seriousness of the problem cannot be underestimated. This is a potentially fatal crisis and does not respond to reassurance or kindly injunctions.

Once we have come to the conclusion that the signs tell us a story with such serious consequences, we must investigate so that we can make an intervention that will be effective. Listening to the parent, even though we may have spontaneous feelings of revulsion, is absolutely essential. The parents may really want help but may not know how to ask for it except indirectly. This is the opportunity to provide it, but we will almost surely fail if we assume a critical attitude and alienate the parents from even a brief relationship with us.

Nor do we need, at this stage, to determine, if there are two parents, which one is responsible for the actual abuse. This can be handled by others. Once we have established some, even slim therapeutic contact with the parents we should act without hesitation by calling in those with experience in this particular problem area.

The best resource for the emergency helper is the Child Welfare Service. Many states have toll-free hot lines for contacting those who can follow-up once a child abuse case has been identified. Since nonprofessionals may become involved at almost any point in the critical arc of abuse, they should make prompt use of these reporting and referral agencies. That is their best service once they have established a "holding" relationship with the involved parents.

In most states, those who report child abuse may remain anonymous, but any report gains in credibility if the one who makes it also reports his or her name. Professionals, or those assisting in a professional setting, are required by law to report evidence of child abuse in many states. These laws, which have been the subject of much debate and discussion, usually grant the reporter confidentiality as well as immunity from prosecution. Emergency counselors should become aware of the availability of services and the legal requirements of the states in which they live and work. Even if such protective provisions do not obtain in a helper's state, it is wise to become familiar with the basics of the child-abuse laws and the accepted reporting procedures of the locality.

In these situations, the emergency helper should also follow up rather than just turn away once a referral seems to have been made. It is easy for a pastor, a teacher, or a doctor to look in again on parents who have revealed this problem, in one way or another, to them. It may happen that the parents, precisely because of their immaturity, do not follow through but merely mire themselves further in the never-ending cycle of abuse. If the emergency worker does not follow up, nobody else may have the knowledge or the interest to do so. This can be accomplished without turning oneself into a crusader or a harmful do-gooder. It is, in fact, common sense to follow up on such referrals. There is no substitute for this, at any point, in dealing with such crises.

In general, most state laws mandate a set procedure that must be followed in responding to a child-abuse report. The first step, naturally, is an investigation of the situation. It is estimated that 60 to 70 percent of such investigations uncover genuine child-abuse crises. The intervention that follows is ordinarily made on the basis of the least restrictive alternative that insures the continued safety of the child. Parents are also offered supportive services by a social worker and/or short-term psychotherapy. Temporary foster-placement homes for the children may be necessary while the parents participate in extended treatment. When such parents deny the problem or reject help, civil proceedings may be initiated in order to remove the child to a safe environment. In more serious cases parents have been prosecuted in civil and, sometimes, criminal court.

A FINAL WORD TO HELPERS

Perhaps no human problem tests a helper as keenly as does that of child abuse. Both the helper's character and judgment are severely strained because of the emotional nature of the problem and because of the high stakes that are involved. If the helper is acquainted with the personality profiles of the potential child abuser he or she will be alerted to provide assistance at a point long before the critical juncture of actual abuse is reached.

Emergency helpers who find, for example, that any of the constellations of characteristics are present in the marriage or the personalities of those with whom they work can read these as distant early warnings. They may then be able to arrange for counseling or other support before the cycle of child abuse is initiated. Those who are involved in marriage preparation work will rightly see the opportunity to refer prospective mates to some form of treatment before they settle into a union that has all the ingredients of child-abuse potential. Educators in family-life work will find new motivation for positive, preventive work in building up and supporting family life and providing early help in situations where any of the flags of warning are flying. This is not a new problem. What is new is our understanding of it and our ability to do something constructive even before crises occur.

In the next chapter, we will consider the specific problems connected with the sexual abuse of children.

For Further Reading

Ambrose, B. (ed.) *Child Abuse and Neglect: Social Service Reader,* vol. I and II. New York: State University of New York at Albany, 1977.

Blair, J., and Duncan, D. F. "Life Crisis as a Precursor to Child Abuse," *Public Health Reports* 91 (1976), pp. 110–15.

Ebeling, N. B., and Hill, D. A. (eds.) *Child Abuse: Intervention and Treatment.* Acton, Mass.: Publishing Sciences Group, 1975.

Fontana, V. J., and Besharov, O. J. *The Maltreated Child.* Springfield, Illinois: Charles C. Thomas, 1977.

Kempe, R. S., and Kempe, C. H. *Child Abuse.* Cambridge, Mass.: Harvard University Press, 1978.

Margrain, S. "Battered Children, Their Parents, Treatment and Prevention," *Child Care, Health and Development* 3 (1977), pp. 49–63.

THIRTEEN

Sexual Abuse of the Young

SEXUAL abuse is a subtype of child abuse in general. While there is nothing new about it, there is a growing recognition both by researchers and by the general public of it as a pervasive and complex problem. While we will offer a rough general definition of this problem, it is also important to remember the wide variety of behaviors that may be lumped under this title, not all of which are equally harmful or dangerous.

What is clear about sexual abuse, or even a suggestion or suspicion of its occurrence, is that it can give rise to a serious crisis not only for the child who is involved but also for his or her family, or the significant persons involved when it takes place in an institutional setting. Sexual abuse of children is still an enormously difficult subject for many people to speak about rationally. Hence the heightened importance of the emergency counselor to whom people turn for assistance at the time of such a difficulty.

Teachers and preachers not only need to know what sensible and positive responses they can employ in the actual crisis situation, but they must also possess a certain basic knowledge of the subject in order to make informed judgments and distinctions about the incident under question.

A DEFINITION

We may consider sexual abuse as the involvement of developmentally immature or underage children in sexual activity with adults. This is activity that children cannot fully understand or comprehend and for which they are unable to give informed consent. Physical contact with the child need not take place to constitute abuse.

Ordinarily such abuse is distinguished according to the abuser's relationship to the child. Thus, there is sexual abuse from strangers, who are neither related to nor acquainted with the child. Secondly, there may be acts of abuse committed by nonfamily adults, who are known to the child or the child's parents. Finally, there is incestuous abuse from family members.

The first category of abuse is almost always reported. Such a step is, of course, beneficial in helping the child and the parents work through the crisis that arises with this problem. It is helpful, for example, to allow the parents to vent their feelings away from the child and to encourage a calm discussion of what happened with the child in language that he or she can understand. Frequently, only the emergency helper will have the opportunity, the facilities, or the presence of mind to make such arrangements.

It is often observed that parents who overreact in this crisis tend to direct their feelings, without consciously intending to, toward the child. This, along with trying to scare the child away from strangers, portrayed as mysterious sources of evil, may simply cause more harm to a child who has already suffered enough. Counselors must keep in mind two psychological areas of concern in the child's life: the ability to trust others in the future and the development of healthy adult sexuality.

A TYPICAL CHILDHOOD EXPERIENCE?

Sociologist David Finkelhor of the University of New Hampshire (speaking at a meeting of the American Orthopsychiatric Association) contends that the sexual victimization of children is "fairly widespread and needs to be incorporated into our image of typical developmental experiences in childhood." He emphasized the family aspects of the problem, noting that certain families "seem intimately connected to whether or not a child is vulnerable to this kind of experience."

Citing his own survey of 795 college undergraduates, both male and female, at six New England colleges and universities, Finkelhor found that 19 percent of the women reported sexual victimization as children. In 75 percent of these cases the offending adults were personally acquainted with the child beforehand. Forty-four percent of the sexual abuses were committed by family members, including fathers, grandfathers, brothers, brothers-in-law, and uncles. Twenty-two percent occurred within the nuclear family. While actual intercourse was infrequent, in 40 percent of the cases the older person touched or manipulated the child's genitals or forced the child to touch his own.

Force was used in more than half the cases, usually in terms of threats that something would happen if they did not cooperate. Two-thirds reported the incidents as negative, a quarter of them describing themselves as in shock. But only a little more than a third reported the abuse at the time, feeling that they would be blamed or would suffer retaliation if they said anything. The girls reported the problem twice as often as the boys.

The vulnerable age for such abuse was shortly before puberty, the time, according to Finkelhor's speculation, when the children are given more freedom and independence and when they are beginning their own experimentation with adult sex role behavior. The problem is that they are not mature enough to handle a sexual advance. Citing family background information, Finkelhor noted that girls who had stepfathers had particularly high rates of victimization, although not always at the hands of the stepfather. Girls who never lived with their natural mothers were three times more vulnerable to sexual abuse than girls who did live with their own mothers. The girls whose mothers were frequently ill, poorly educated, or alcoholic were also abused at a higher rate.

This study indicates the dimensions of the problem. Counselors would be naïve, therefore, to think that such occurrences take place only rarely. One of the best ways in which they can prepare to operate effectively in a crisis of sexual child abuse is through having previously worked through their own feelings about this difficult subject.

Helpers should not be surprised to discover that they express emotional distress about a problem that has such a threatening character. By examining these feelings and educating themselves thoroughly on the nature of sexual abuse, counselors may acquire the steady presence that is the foundation for their good judgment and responsible actions in the midst of a crisis of this nature. Dealing effectively with the complexities of sexual child abuse demands realism, but not at the price of surrendering idealism about the growth potential of human beings.

Two Common Problem Areas

The first of these centers on homosexuality, the second on incestuous relationships.

Nobody fully understands homosexuality—or heterosexuality, for that matter—so a common-sense approach is always in order. When a crisis arises it is not the time to politicize the sexual preferences that are involved. Nor is it the occasion for persons to champion their cause through exploiting the misery and suffering of the individuals involved. Any discussion of homosexuality can quickly move in one of these directions. Counselors should see that such theoretical analyses and arguments are postponed until after the crisis is resolved.

What exactly does homosexual contact involve for young people? It is possible that they may have a homosexual teacher who never expresses his or her homosexuality. There is no need, then, to promote a crisis when none exists—except in one's imagination. It is also possible for young children to engage in homoerotic sex play without being perverts and without scarring each other for life. If helpers are contacted about a situation in which, for example, mutual masturbation is discovered, he or she should assess the truth of the matter carefully to minimize the possibility of exaggerating a small, relatively common incident into an unnecessary crisis.

The counselor should not, however, get in the position of seeming to approve or encourage such behavior. As psychiatrists Walter F. Char and John F. McDermott recommend ("Children's Exposure To Homosexuals," *Medical Aspects of Human Sexuality*), "a matter-of-fact 'that's enough' is the best parental approach." They note, however, the danger involved if "an adolescent with a fixed homosexual orientation . . . imposes his will on a younger child over a period of time." Obviously, this is more serious, and the counselor should work toward making appropriate referrals for both parties.

Adult homosexual seduction is something else, although, here again, some distinctions must be kept in mind. Seductive maneuvers vary in intensity and consequences. So a child who is invoved in a minor incident in which he or she is not active will probably not suffer much harm. The child's reaction, for example, to having a hand put on his or her leg in a theater or on a bus, should be explored, again in a calm and sensible way. As Char and Burns observe, "such a sexual incident tends to make a child feel that something 'wrong,' 'dirty,' and 'illicit' had occurred which might cause him anxiety and confusion. The child needs common sense explanations and warm parental support."

So, too, the man involved should not be treated like a criminal but should be dealt with clearly and firmly. Counselors should be wary of too readily accepting excuses from offenders. "I was drinking" is one of the favorites. Some steps should be taken to see that the person gets help and does not get back into the position of trust or easy access to the young in which the incident occurred. Ordinarily the child will be able to work his or her way out of the situation without further help, although help may be necessary if the child evidences psychiatric symptoms later on.

Suppose it is not a single, passing occurrence. Suppose the parents discover that there has been sustained seduction. This calls for professional assistance, and the intervening helper should establish referral as a clear goal in resolving the crisis that attends the discovery of such behavior. Younger children are particularly vulnerable to seduction by older, stronger persons, often male relatives who exact promises of secrecy from them. This can cause serious complications, and in sorting out the pieces in such a critical incident, the counselor should not shrug off the effects, which, for the undeveloped, may be seriously damaging.

Burns and Char also discuss "aggressive homosexual attack," something which, "although not common . . . is very dangerous. It not only brings to bear the problem of homosexuality, but also aggression, violence, threatening the child's emotional health and physical being." Obviously helpers must assist in making prompt psychiatric referrals in such incidents.

Often the child reveals the homosexual attack to the helper in the latter's role as trusted pastor or teacher. The counselor should be calm and gentle, allowing the child to express himself as fully as possible. It is enormously important for him to feel that the counselor, as a trusted adult, understands, believes, and stands with him. Much healing can be accomplished before the counselor has to deal with the parents or the offender. Naturally, if helpers observe any serious psychiatric symptoms, they should arrange for professional assistance immediately.

INCEST

Once again, the first challenge for emergency helpers is to define the situation accurately. To this end, they may well follow the recommendations of psychiatrist Frank S. Pittman, III ("Counseling Incestuous Families," *Medical Aspects of Human Sexuality*). As Pittman notes, the problem may be real or imaginary, but a report by a child of incest or attempted incest should be taken seriously because, even if the incest is imagined, "the sense of sexual threat and perhaps a breach in generational boundaries are real." The counselor should be aware of this and not just dismiss the situation because "nothing really happened."

The child, as Pittman observes, may be asking for protection, for the maintenance of the protected child role in the family, or may be demanding "that the informed parent act in a parental and sexually adult manner." Sometimes the parent who is not involved wants to ignore the situation in order "to avoid a crisis which is seriously pathological in its parental and sexual functioning."

The worst harm occurs when the child must keep the secret of an incestuous relationship in a family system that, for whatever reason, is content to live with the abuse rather than to correct it. Nothing can be resolved, as Pittman says, unless at least three people are involved, "the victim, the accused, and the displaced parent, who is both the 'cuckold' and the failed protector." Others may have to be involved before the crisis can be resolved and proper help obtained. For example, other children who may become victims or whose well-being is affected by the presence of the problem may have to be dealt with.

Recurrent incest is clearly a far more serious problem than a one-time occurrence, which may be motivated by distinctive pathology, such as psychosis in the offending parent. As Pittman summarizes the situation, "If the child continues the incest or fails to report it, something is wrong with the child's relationship with the uninvolved parent. If the uninvolved parent fails to act, it is clear that such a person is dynamically linked to the problem." There is, in such chronic situations, an emotional affliction that affects both parents.

Typically, the father becomes sexually involved with the daughter if the mother, because of her own pathology, has rejected her role as wife to her husband and mother to her daughter. The low-level problems of such mothers are numerous and match in a certain way the pathology of the father, who is frequently psychotic and often an alcoholic. The inner psychological dynamics of such families are entwined like complex electronic circuitry. One part of what is wrong cannot be treated in isolation from the other significant family members.

THE COUNSELOR'S CHOICES

In such a situation, which frequently peaks in a bizarre crisis, counselors want to avoid interventions aimed at blaming or punishing any member of the family. Only if there is a threat of violence or rape should the intervening counselor act swiftly to change the situation by separating family members for a time. But this can only be a prelude to ongoing treatment.

To choose the proper treatment, the counselor should evaluate, as Dr. Pittman suggests, "not just the incestuous parent, but all three relevant members."

The next decision that must be made concerns a judgment on whether this is a classic incestuous family or whether it is a one-time event related to one family member's psychological problems. Evaluating those involved may lead to the diagnosis of severe mental and emotional problems in any or all of the family members. Obviously, emergency counselors cannot attempt to treat long-standing difficulties of this nature. They need to know the degree of pathology, however, in order to take the next step, which may be the recommendation of family therapy.

This may be carried out "in conjunction with individual therapy for one or more family members," which can be worked out with the professionals to whom the members of the family are referred. In a crisis, the vital thing is to get the process of referral moving. In the family in which incest is a long-standing and deeply-rooted problem, the overall pathology as well as the individual difficulties of family members will require ongoing treatment.

It is wise for helpers to recall Pittman's injunction: "Aside from the disorder in family relationships and the paralysis of a guilty secret, the most destructive aspect of incest is the furor it produces. To prevent this, the therapist must keep his sense of alarm under control and encourage the family members to do so."

SIGNALS

Helpers in various professions should also be alert to some of the diagnostic signs of sexual abuse in children:

0–5 years—States of fear; night terrors; clinging behavior; developmental regression.

5–11 years—Sudden anxiety attacks; intense fears; depression; insomnia; weight loss or gain; truancy; school failure.

adolescents—serious rebellion against the mother or parent of the opposite sex, who is seen as having failed to protect the child; a daughter who is assigned more and more maternal functions; serious delinquency; severe loss of self-esteem; runaway behavior; depression; suicidal attempts.

Treatment of incest victims may be long and arduous. It is almost always necessary to eliminate contact between the parent and child through voluntary or legal sanctions.

In summary, child abuse is a serious problem in this country and is only now receiving the clinical attention it deserves. Research on child abuse has generated some solid results, and it seems that some form of supportive therapy can help in many cases. Sexual abuse has received much less attention. The research that has occurred seems to focus on the treatment of the offender rather than on the victim.

Despite tough legislation concerning child-abuse reporting and investigation, the actual delivery of services to ensure the child's safety is subject to some of the worst inadequacies of any of the social service bureaucracies. This sad reality only serves to increase the responsibility and obligation of the helper who suspects an abusive situation.

For Further Reading

Char, Walter F., and McDermott, John F. "Children's Exposure to Homosexuals," *Medical Aspects of Human Sexuality* (Aug. 1977), p. 81.

Pittman, Frank S. "Counseling Incestuous Families," *Medical Aspects of Human Sexuality* (April 1976), pp. 57–58.

The following helpful booklets may be obtained from the National Committee for the Prevention of Child Abuse, Suite 510, 111 East Wacker Drive, Chicago, IL 60601: *Basic Facts About Child Abuse, Dealing with Sexual Child Abuse,* and Hay, J. Gary, M.D., *Understanding Sexual Child Abuse.*

FOURTEEN

When Disaster Strikes

SOME helpers feel that every day is a disaster of sorts. And it is certainly true that the steady drain on a counselor's energies by routine difficulties falling in unpredictable patterns can make life seem as if it were being lived inside a whirlwind. But these everyday problems, however tragic, are on a manageable and imaginable scale. A full-blown disaster apes the critical nature of every other problem but explodes as if from within with a force and shape that can be truly overwhelming and disordering. In the amount of damage done and the number of lives affected, full-scale disasters are difficult even for those close to them to describe; they are enveloping and often change the course of people's lives. And yet these too have characteristic phases and typical reaction patterns that can be studied in advance, so that counselors with a capacity to read their signs, the way they can read the unconscious language of mourning, can learn how to use their own strengths most effectively when a major problem strikes.

WHAT IS A DISASTER?

Researchers who have attempted an abstract definition of the impact of a hurricane, a large fire, flood, or other serious large-scale problem, emphasize certain features they have in common. It is, as Naomi Golan puts it, "a collective stress situation" (*Treatment in Crisis Situations*). It affects many members of an interlocking social system, who lose both the shield of the ordinary conditions of life, such as safety in the physical environment and freedom from attack, and the staples of income, shelter, and nourishment. A key element in a disaster is that the afflicted person is deprived of the ordinary guidance and information that they need to carry on their everyday activities. Life is out of joint, and anything can happen in the strange void that settles on the disaster victims.

Disasters can be of the external variety, such as floods and earthquakes; they may also be events that are largely internal, although just as dislocating, such as depressions, strikes, riots, civil uprisings, and political breakdowns. Some disasters, though they leave no physical wreckage, are nevertheless enormously devastating in their effects.

Whatever the nature of the disaster, it threatens the self-image of those affected by it. Such a threat is intertwined with challenges to the supporting social system, the life goals of those involved, and the values or the beliefs that govern their lives. Disasters demand responses that are distorted from those of ordinary life. They may press people to expand or restrict their regular functioning because the ways in which persons ordinarily handle difficulties are no longer adequate. Both individuals and groups as well as the institutions with which they are familiar lose their balance and are unable to function effectively. The stores are closed, there is no place to get money, the ordinary means of transportation and the ordinary supports of human relationship are withdrawn.

The grim equality of disasters rests on the fact that they spare nobody; the community and each individual is subjected to hardship of one kind or another. This very truth calls into being a "community of sufferers" that can prove to be of immense importance in providing help and bringing some eventual healing to those who were afflicted but who went through it together.

CAN YOU PREDICT THEM?

Some disasters are totally unexpected, as, for example, when a presumably safe scene suddenly turns into tragedy because of a flaw that nobody anticipated or expected. When there is a major accident at a construction site, such as the collapse of a scaffold during the construction of a cooling tower at Willow Island, West Virginia, in 1978, in which 51 men were killed instantly, there is no expectation of disaster and no way to prepare for it. In other situations, such as the approach of funnel clouds or the slow crawl of a storm toward a coastline, discrete phases may be identified.

The warning phase is marked by some heightened anxiety and apprehension, but most people continue to function normally, going about their business while checking on their radios or in some other way for the latest news. This heightened vigilance may also be characterized by a need for exchanging reassurances with friends and neighbors. A mood of foreboding, is, however, clearly present. As researchers have noted, people who may be involved in a disaster need to put forth some effort to keep themselves ready to react sensibly during this time. As Golan puts it, there is need for an "optimal level of stress," a keenness of attention to the signs and symbols, such as flags of warning, that tell the story of the storm's progress.

The time of threat is that period during which the danger is imminent and inevitable. The threat of disaster is no longer general or slightly vague. It seems to be aimed directly at the individual and his locality; the problem becomes an intensely personal one. During this time, when the disaster is about to strike, people tend to react rather individualistically. Families gather together, and there may be some evidence of panic at the prospect of the imminent hazard. If people do something at this time, even though it may not ultimately be very effective, they feel less vulnerable and less impotent.

WHEN THE DISASTER STRIKES

The actual impact of the disaster finds the victims acting in highly predictable, if somewhat surprising, ways. Some people are emotionally overwhelmed and only slowly pull themselves out of it. This is not true, however, of most people, who although they exhibit the signs of shock—lack of emotion, low stimulation level, low activity, undemandingness and docility—do not collapse; in short order, as a matter of fact, they are able to participate fully in repair and restoration efforts.

Perhaps the most surprising aspect of reaction to disasters is the small amount of panic that ensues. Disaster movies are filled with it but ordinary people are more resilient than screenwriters suppose. It is important for helpers involved in crises to realize this lest they spend their efforts needlessly trying to avert panic that does not occur. It is also helpful to understand that after victims recover from their initial sense that the storm or accident was designed expressly for them and their family, they are capable of and generally do exhibit strong impulses to help others. At such points those involved in the disaster are capable of the heroic feats of strength and endurance that are well beyond them in ordinary circumstances. Thus, at the disaster at Willow Island, fellow workers of the 51 men buried under the rubble of the collapsed scaffolding were able to lift heavy sections of iron without apparent effort in order to free the victims. Every disaster is the scene of comparable activities; sometimes it can be observed in the long, grueling hours of less dramatic work of which ordinary people are capable at such times.

After the impact the helper may think that all the moving about is at random or just represents dazed people who don't know what they are doing. Analyses of such activity, however, reveal that it is far from chaotic and that very little of it is purposeless. Because the ordinary frame and setting for human activity has shifted so radically it is difficult to pick up the pattern of constructive activity that is actually present. It is also a time in which the morale of people who have shared the same affliction is high and during which they are capable of responding to sensible leadership and direction for their activities.

Helpers should also understand something about leadership that is manifest at this time. Natural leaders emerge to take charge of the group, which responds willingly to their directions. These leaders may not match the pattern of presumed leadership that existed before the disaster struck, nor does it necessarily follow along the lines of age, occupation, or social class. These people remain calm, seem to have an instinct for what to do, and prove to be able managers of the many problems that arise. Obviously, helpers who have these natural qualities should use them to their fullest. In any case they should be able to recognize those who have these instincts and join with them in marshalling the energies of the larger groups of victims for the work to be done.

CHECKING IT OUT

The inventory period follows the main brunt of the disaster; during this time some survey is made of the actual extent of the damage. Because rumors can fly at these times, a rapid and accurate appraisal of exactly what has occurred is absolutely essential. During this time some of the afflicted will begin to evidence physical complaints of varied kinds or may seem to withdraw from reality through fantasies and delusions. This is also the period for anger, depression, and the effects of the social disintegration caused by the accident or storm.

Most people, however, will make good progress in shaking off the impact of the problem and will return to their predisaster level of functioning. Others, of course, will not make a complete recovery and will emerge with some residual problems.

This is followed by periods of rescue and remedy in which the problems of dealing with the aftermath are paramount in the concern of rescue workers. Remedying the problems may constitute the longest phase of reaction to a disaster. It involves the victims in something that few of them anticipate but a reality for which helpers, especially those who come from outside, must themselves be prepared. Because there is a build-up of spirit and morale among the cooperating victims of a disaster they may resent help, even though it is very much needed, that comes from the outside. The reasons for this are not completely understood, but there is no doubt about the reality of this reaction. It adds to the difficulties of the helpers, who may have come long distances with badly needed supplies. A local helper, aware of this complication, may help to mediate it as well as assist the outsiders through moral support and by helping them to understand that this is a somewhat expected human reaction.

A specialized feature of disasters is the descent of the media, its members under great pressure, not to help the victims, but to file a story by deadline. They can often, even unwittingly, cause further dislocation and emotional harm to the already upset victims of the disaster. At the Willow Island disaster, for example, such harsh resentment developed against the press that the police finally made a statement that they could not guarantee the reporters' safety any longer. However, because of the natural leadership of the mayor of the small community of Belmont, and the cooperation of others, the press were restricted both at the accident site and at the temporary morgue set up for the identification of bodies. Disaster in contemporary society means tragedy for those on the inside, but for many others, especially media members, it means spectacle that has to be "covered." Some anticipation of the problems of managing aggressive news reporters should be an aspect of every disaster plan.

POINTERS FOR HELPERS

It is admittedly difficult to comprehend the nature of a disaster with any kind of accuracy or in any real perspective until a long time afterward. Helpers who find themselves involved in serious and traumatic events can, however, remember certain basic notions that will help them in whatever work they do in response to the problem.

First of all, counselors should work to avoid being overwhelmed by the magnitude of the disaster. To do this, we may have to limit the range of our activity and discipline ourselves only to provide assistance that is sensible and truly feasible in the circumstances. For example, assistance must be given on the basis of need, and someone, like a *triage* officer, must make these decisions without agonizing debate or delay. This keeps the whole response moving in an orderly fashion.

Gathering accurate information and getting it out is an enormously important aspect of reacting to a disaster. Families need and should get accurate information as soon as possible about the status of one of their members who may be involved in the accident or disaster. Keeping records and reports in order is indispensable so that this information can be transmitted simply and accurately. Families may be split up by the occurrence of a disaster, and the need to keep them informed about each other's whereabouts is extremely important in moderating their psychological reactions. An added common sense aspect of this, of course, is to get members of families together again as soon as possible. The family's continuing value as a source of support and meaning emerges clearly at a time of disaster.

In the same way, helpers should try to mobilize survivors to involve themselves in clean-up or other necessary activities. That is good for their psychological well-being. Sometimes they are immobilized until a helper can get them back on the track, getting them, for example, to follow the outlines of their daily schedule.

Alienation and a feeling of not belonging anywhere are sometimes the outcomes of a disaster in which massive social fragmentation has taken place. Helpers should try to get people who have been displaced by the event in touch with neighbors or other family members. Separating persons too far from what is familiar to them can be disconcerting, to say the least. Common sense dictates the rebuilding of a family and other community units as swiftly as possible.

The helper, even the person without extensive training, can be very useful in assisting those persons who react with the "disaster syndrome," the temporary withdrawal and paralysis that was described earlier. Recognizing that this is not a serious or permanent problem, helpers can reassure and explain to the individuals something about the nature of what they are experiencing. This provides a structure that is extremely helpful to the individual so afflicted, as does the design and follow-up supervision of such minor tasks of which they may be capable. Persons who evince major symptoms of psychiatric disturbance should, however, be treated, if possible, by whichever competent professional may be in service at the scene.

People in a crisis caused by a disaster do not need a Pollyanna filled with mindless reassurance. They are helped much more by those who can assist them in making a realistic appraisal of exactly what has occurred; this becomes the basis for their future responses. Many people speculate about the effects of a disaster without really finding out what they are. They frequently overestimate the problems and underestimate their own capacity to respond rationally to them.

A corollary to this, of course, is that helpers should avoid giving false reassurances to people when they have no solid information to support them. Most people would like to believe that everything is all right, that all their loved ones are safe, and that they have suffered no permanent damage to their property. To falsely lead people to believe that this will indeed be the outcome leaves them unprepared for a realistic view of what has actually occurred. Only if they can squarely face the possibilities can they draw upon their own inner strength to make the adjustments necessary in a world that, for them, may never be the same again.

A delicate area for some people is their becoming dependent on a helper for some periods after a serious accident or storm. Naturally, it is never good for a helper to let this happen, but allowing it for brief periods and with an understanding of what is happening can be therapeutic.

Clergymen may have many official duties to carry out at the scene of a disaster but they, along with teachers and other professionals, may also possess the mantle of authority that allows them to offer support to rescue workers who may be suffering because of the strain of the work that is demanded of them. It may fall to the nonprofessional helper to see that workers take breaks, that they get fed, and that some scheduling is set up to make sure that they are used sensibly and are not overtaxed by the stress of the situation.

PREPARATION

Many hospitals and communities have regular drills, made as realistic as possible, in order to prepare workers for the mood and stress of an actual disaster. Nonmedical specialists may seldom think of doing the same thing, but according to most research, it is the most sensible preparation for the problems of a disaster that we know of. To take but one example, how well prepared would the staff of a local church be to respond to a disaster, whether it be a storm, an accident, or a misbehaving nuclear reactor? How can the services of the clergy, to cite just this one profession, best be put at the disposal of the victims? How could the church building be used, what place might there be for emergency religious services, and so forth.

At the time of the Willow Island disaster, an emergency plan involving members of the clergy was put into effect almost immediately after the accident occurred. Clergy were assigned to accompany the relatives to the temporary morgue, to sit with them while they waited to identify the bodies, and to accompany them to their homes. They served as escorts and counselors, offering support but not intruding excessively. This was maintained throughout the difficult weekend and provides a good example of how nonprofessionals, with some preparation, can offer sensible assistance at a time of major trauma. Perhaps each parish team, or each faculty group, could rehearse the steps they would take and the roles they would play if they suddenly became involved in a major disaster.

For Further Reading

Baker, G. W. and Chapman, D. W., (eds.) *Man and Society in Disaster*. New York: Basic Books, 1962.

Barton, Allen. *Communities in Disaster*. New York: Doubleday 1969.

Golan, Naomi, *Treatment in Crisis Situations*. The Free Press, 1978, p. 125.

Parad, Howard J., et al, (eds.) *Emergency and Disaster Management*. Bowie, Md.: Charles Press, 1976.

Quarentellu, E. and Dynes, R. "When Disaster Strikes," *Psychology Today* 9 (1972), pp. 67–70.

Resnik, H., and Ruben, H. *Emergency Psychiatric Care*. Bowie, Md.: Charles Press, 1975.

FIFTEEN

Life Changes

To make "passages," to experience "midlife changes," even to get a divorce: these have become part of the current American consciousness about what people not only may but should do during their middle years. It has become almost fashionable to pass through the valley of critical transition and to climb up the far slope as a changed person. The massive amount of writing and research, not to mention newspaper and television features, centering on the varied bridges and links between the phases of adult growth have made people intensely aware of what is happening to them as they age, shift jobs, or find their perspectives on life transforming.

The phenomenon of self-concern that is demonstrated in all this does not surprise us in a psychologically-minded age. The metaphors that have been provided for contemporary Americans do say something truthful about the challenges and presumed rewards of aging. The effect, of course, like that of the right word used by a therapist, is that people recognize their own experience much better; they know that they are on a passage, and they can number the challenges they must face. While these were once described chiefly in literature, they are now the stuff of late-night interviews and situation comedies. America is watching itself grow old, and if not particularly enjoying it, at least has some notion of what is happening to it.

This does not mean that we are inventing crises for ourselves. One of the luxuries of an advanced society is that it has the leisure to name its experiences and to deal with them at a depth that was impossible in previous, more crowded times. Similarly, for example, it is said that adolescence was discovered only after the conditions of society changed so that children were not immediately apprenticed into trades where the work they took on masked the developmental changes that were occurring within them.

A few years ago, Dr. Kenneth Keniston of Yale University suggested that a new life phase that might be termed "youth" had clearly emerged between adolescence and adulthood, again because of vastly changed social conditions. Now, as the nation grows biologically older, its citizens have a much better sense of the growth problems of middle age, of, in other words, the long, unfolding crisis that is life itself. Clergymen, physicians, educators, and even lawyers are witnesses, in various ways, to the phenomenon of the long, curling wave of these changes as it breaks across the lives of those with whom they deal every day. Indeed, they may know the pressure first-hand in their own lives.

While transitional crises are hardly the well-defined and urgent emergencies that are the usual focus of those who must intervene when there is an accident or a personal disaster of some kind, they are filled with tensions and challenges that test a helper's capacities to be effective. Periods of adjustment can be truly critical in nature, and the assistance of a wise and patient helper can make a significant difference in the lives of those who experience them.

Perhaps the wise counselor needs some philosophical grounding as well as some familiarity with at least the popular literature that reflects the difficulties particular to certain times in the life history of the average person. First of all, there may be no specific treatment, much less cure, for the difficulties that accompany each phase of human development. An understanding perspective, rooted in accurate information, is the best resource for helpers who find themselves party to the distress of some client or colleague. They should restrain their interventions, be wary of gimmicky suggestions, and strive to see the affected person or family as unique rather than as like something in a textbook.

In addition to a broad, informed view of these phases, one needs a certain familiarity with the special language in which the crisis may express itself. We will return to this shortly; it is enough to remember that the special voice of the crisis is symbolic and that it rises from the unconscious level of the personality. It is not, in other words, a logical or orderly self-presentation; transitional problems break into the open only in disguise.

It is also helpful to recall that there may be specific challenges—things that must be done both emotionally and in the physical world—in order to work through various periods of transition. A person may have to take concrete actions, in other words, to implement the decisions that, like it or not, must be made during these times. Of course, the nature of the action differs greatly from one stage to another, but some sense of the need to move practically is essential for the successful resolution of the critical period. People do not, in other words, dream their way out of these problems.

WHAT DO THEY INVOLVE?

Life crises hardly ever concern themselves only with one person. They always affect some network of relationships; the people around the affected person feel the effects of the turmoil within the central individual in the crisis. Sometimes it is a system of relationships, such as the family, that experiences the transitional conflict. Sometimes it is just one member of the family whose crisis distends the normal functioning of the surrounding social or work group. Getting a fix on the total nature of the adjustment conflict is the first order of business for helpers who, because of their profession, find themselves involved in the life crises of others all the time. Thus, for example, Scherz ("The Crisis of Adolescence in Family Life," *Social Casework*) writes of the "universal psychological tasks" that face the family and any individual member in it during the various life-stage challenges. She lists the family's tasks as being:

1. Those centering on the conflict between emotional separation and interdependence, or connectedness.
2. Self-autonomy in conflict with responsibility for others.
3. The ever-present tension between closeness, or intimacy, and distance.

The individual family member, subject of the same intruding life-stage crisis, may find challenges focused in a slightly different way. These include:

1. The need for facing separation and the effective resolution of dependency needs.
2. The need to deal with intimacy and to develop a healthy sexual identity.
3. The development of autonomy and a healthy respect for the self.

These are reciprocal aspects of the same overall situation. A family experiences a crisis as a unit, but each member experiences it in a particular way. The same thing may be said of other social systems. It would be foolish for people to ignore or to treat cavalierly the crises of transition that occur when a business reorganizes itself, shifts location, or reexamines its purposes and goals. Members of Catholic religious communities underwent severe transitional crises during the past decade as the changes that occurred in the Church posed first one challenge to the adaptive capacity of the group and then another, related but slightly different, for each individual member.

This is such a commonsensical and fundamental truth that we do not want to obscure it with too much jargon. Yet counselors cannot provide much assistance unless they can perceive and identify correctly the relevant elements in this pervasive two-tier reaction. That is what occurs when a family or group member becomes ill—or sometimes even when someone takes a vacation—or when a family member dies or moves to another locality. These examples could be multiplied endlessly.

Crises of transition cram the everyday life of Americans; they are not casual, and they involve the whole system as well as individual members. No response that does not acknowledge this can prove to be effective in the long run.

What Can You Do?

If we are proposing that members of every profession, except perhaps diamond cutters or other such possessors of necessarily individualized and isolating skills, are awash in transitional crises every day, then what can we do about those who are suffering through them?

The first injunction remains, as always, that of patient understanding. This is very different from jumping to hasty conclusions with prefabricated solutions. Nor does it indicate standing by and doing nothing; rather, it demands the most exquisite concentration of one's attention and sensitivity on the problem that is at the center of the stage. This is the point at which our capacity to hear and translate the symbolic language of the transitional crisis is most sharply challenged.

For example, when there is trouble in a family, when, for example, the oldest son, formerly a good and dutiful student, suddenly grows indifferent and negativistic about school, the counselor understands that the youth is expressing some hurt or problem in the symbolic language of acting out. The young person does not understand fully what he is doing; he cannot easily express it to himself or others or else the problem would not have assumed the shape that it has.

What, the helper asks, is going on in the family, or in the individual's relationship to it, that is generating this reaction? While the cause may differ markedly from situation to situation, it may not be too difficult to identify it if we take the time and make the effort to do so. A serious problem in the relationship of the parents may radiate out into the behavior of the adolescent, who is thrown for a loss by this sudden shift in his experience of his family. The sickness, or near death, of a parent may send the same waves rolling through a household, each member's reaction telling something about their individuality and the complexity of the unit's interrelationships.

Symbolic reactions need gentle translation even for those who are involved in them. This is one function that the helper can exercise very well, especially if he or she has the confidence of the affected person and some access to the family itself. An outsider may be especially helpful because the parents may, in their own middle age, be facing unexpected crises just at the time their adolescent children are facing the challenges of school or career choice. The interaction of two sets of transitional crises may have a strong impact on all family members. But the crisis will surface as a school problem because that is something that is easier to deal with than digging into and understanding in depth the emotional exchanges that are taking place within and between family members.

It is important to recognize that we are not talking about families ridden with serious psychological difficulties. There is nothing necessarily pathological about this acting out, which reflects and symbolizes the stresses of a family in the grip of transition. These are garden-variety problems that show up regularly in the best ordered households, sometimes precisely because they are so well-ordered and therefore so filled with expectation on the behavior of the family. Naturally, any sensible counselor will seek referral for family therapy or for individual professional treatment if serious psychopathology is present. But in many situations the amateur can intervene in the developmental crisis and provide sensible and effective assistance.

The possibility of educating an otherwise healthy family is, of course, very real; it can go a long way in helping to resolve the difficulties that are the signs of the adjustment period being undergone by everyone. No matter what the acting out looks like—drug-taking, a car accident, even a pregnancy—wise and understanding counselors can help persons to see that it is not the end of the world and that they should not focus excessively on the symptom when they may be able to proceed directly to an examination of the underlying cause.

Helpers can easily explain the fact that such problems are hardly unique and that they cannot be solved in isolation from the roots that they have in other, more inclusive, family experiences. It is always supportive to a family when they can see that they are not alone in going through a problem. That does not solve the difficulty, of course, but it lessens alienation considerably and allows family members to feel that they are not so different from the rest of humanity. It is the unfortunate focusing on the symptom, that is, on doing something to stop the acting out without doing something to eradicate its cause, that may worsen transitional crises that otherwise might be handled, if not without pain, at least without additional and totally unnecessary suffering.

If we reflect on it, most of us can identify periods during which we acted out, or expressed symbolically, some conflict connected with our changing life or with the changing life of our family. Many of the events that are perceived as problems in and by themselves are actually the signals of an underlying process. When we understand the process, we may be able to bear its pressure better, making further modification in our activities that can have a very beneficial effect on those caught in the crisis.

Thus, for example, a readjustment of a family schedule that allows a mother or father to be home when the children come back from school may have an almost startling effect in resolving the conflicted behavior of a child who has had no other way of manifesting feelings of rejection or isolation than through behavioral troubles at school.

The same can be said of a wide variety of transitional crises. What is it attached to and what is it really expressing about the person who is in the middle of it? Helping the person to ask these questions, or at least to explore the way to phrase them, even tentatively, can provide the vehicle for self-understanding that may allow the crisis to be resolved.

It may well be that the individual who feels trapped in a classic midlife crisis finds little help in reading or rereading the many descriptions, however accurate, of his or her plight. Neither should such persons feel that they must move toward the culturally popular solution to the problem. They may not have to change their job, move to another locale, or entertain the notion of divorce. With the assistance of a patient counselor they may be able to see into the causes of their discontent, and even if they cannot change them completely, they may be able to change themselves or make other adjustments that enable them to work through the challenges satisfactorily.

OTHER POINTS TO REMEMBER

Helping people to look more broadly at their life situations is very different from giving them popular and pat answers. Such answers, like the familiar reassurances, often just convince the troubled person that we do not understand the particulars of their crisis.

Helpers should at least familiarize themselves with the popular psychological literature that is concerned with life transitions. This will help them to appreciate the vocabulary that those in crisis may use to describe themselves, which is frequently taken from such literature.

Those who find themselves as attendants at some crisis of transition should understand the ways in which crises, which often seem very different, are similar to each other. For example, each crisis has a life of its own, with phases that can be charted fairly clearly. We must allow people to work through their individual periods of crisis in their own way. We cannot do it for them, no matter how much we might wish that we could. Besides, we would only be interfering with a natural and absolutely essential process if we were to do so.

We must let people mourn, we must permit them to search, even symbolically, for the pieces of their lives or careers that they want to put together in a new fashion.

Expect people to be different as they emerge on the other side of the transition. These times of crises have a psychological logic about them; they are meant to be times of growth, of shedding past solutions and trying new ones, of consolidating the personality, of shaping a new sense of the self, as, for example, after the death of a loved one, so that one can return to a useful and satisfying life in a new manner. Let the wife learn what she must do to put her grief behind her, so that she can live and function as a widow. Let the adolescent work through the difficult issues, so that he or she can put adolescence successfully behind. Do not try to delay crises, just aim at helping people successfully work through them.

It is also helpful always to remember that no resolution of a crisis is ever completely successful, that scars of one sort of another will remain. There are, no perfect ways of resolving any kind of emergency, because, by their nature, they destabilize our lives and demand that we rebuild them. Perhaps no people are more involved or more helpful in working these through than the teachers, ministers, and dozens of others who have such intimate access to individuals and families as they face the never-ending crises of adjustment.

For Further Reading

Bell, Robert. *Marriage and Family Interaction,* 3rd ed. Homewood, Ill.: Dorsey Press, 1971.

Erikson, Erik H. *Identify and the Life Cycle*. New York: International Universities Press, 1959.

Fried, Barbara. *The Middle-Aged Crisis*. New York: Harper & Row, 1976.

Glick, I., Weiss, R., and Parkes, C. M., *The First Year of Bereavement*. New York: John Wiley & Sons, 1974.

Scherz, Frances H., "The Crisis of Adolescence in Family Life," *Social Casework* 48 (April 1967), pp. 209–15.

Sheehy, Gail. *Passages*. New York: E. P. Dutton, 1976. (1977, Bantam, paper).

SIXTEEN

Subtle Emergencies

MANY social observers have begun to step back and to examine more closely the nature of the journey Americans have been on for nearly a generation. Everybody is familiar with its main feature—the exaltation of individual freedom and rights and the concomitant decline of the institutions, such as marriage, that once limited these with a view toward maintaining stability and continuity for society at large.

Thus, in a way that was by no means totally unhealthy or misguided, the formerly strict social proscription of divorce and remarriage has been modified considerably. There has been a general recognition that not all marriages were necessarily marriages in the first place and that men and women who made life hell for each other and their children could choose another course beyond that of gritting their teeth and bearing it.

As in all massive social shifts, however, the extreme has also been touched, by those who have used divorce as a solution to problems that were not totally insoluble and, in themselves, need not have indicated separation or the termination of the marriage relationship. Divorce has, for some, become almost an automatic option when marriage difficulties rise.

Indeed, divorce has been transformed from an experience that might render a person socially unacceptable to one that may be the hallmark of an enlightened and fashionable mentality. Few are unfamiliar with the divorce rate that now claims a third of first marriages and 40 percent of second marriages. While social observers may argue over the ultimate significance of these facts, there is no question that marriage has suffered a crisis of confidence and stability.

What has this to do with the person who may be called in at the time of an emergency? The clergy, teachers, lawyers, and even counselors with extensive training are in contact every day with the subtle crises that bubble up because of the increased pressures that may be found in contemporary marriage. While we will discuss the crisis nature of divorce in a later chapter, we focus now on the minicrises that may go unrecognized, be poorly identified, or, all too often, be given improper treatment by those who wish to be of assistance.

It's in the Air

The acceptability of separation and divorce is an exacerbating condition for couples who find their lives together stressful. Divorce, while it has seemed a welcome answer for many who felt it was an impossible option before, has also become a magnet, pulling at and distorting into emergencies situations that may not necessarily point to a bad relationship or to a need for dissolution.

When something is in the air the way divorce is at the present time, helpers who stand on the front lines of life's battleground need to be able to sort out the nature of the struggles before them. Is it hand-to-hand combat to the death? Or are these people fighting out of misunderstanding or over the wrong issue? Peace may still be possible, not at any price but through a compromise that may be satisfactory, as well as healthy, for both sides.

Another Change

There are also fashions in symptoms and the structure of emotional diseases. While the Victorian era was familiar with hysterical paralyses and blindness as the surface expressions of internal conflicts that could not be faced or dealt with in any other way, the present age has witnessed a projection of intrapsychic problems in quite a different manner. As psychiatrist Frederic Flach has noted ("Marriage: New Therapeutic Dimensions," *Psychiatric Annals* 7:6 (June 1979), p. 14), those inner problems that were once acted out by social withdrawal or experiences of despair are presently observed in a transformed fashion. People with such problems "can be seen as experiencing those conflicts in terms of immediate, critical life situation problems," in "specific external dilemmas, the solution to which (they) cannot seem to work out . . ."

In other words, individuals who have problems within their own psychological structure now tend to displace the underlying conflict into something outside of themselves, into a problem at work, for example, or, more commonly, into a problem with a spouse or a friend. What appears to be a signal of a marriage problem may in reality be the sign of something different; correct assessment and treatment of the problem is essential, therefore, because it constitutes, in marriage at least, a real and present emergency.

Divorce is no solution for a person whose own depression is the cause of the critical incident in the marriage relationship. Those who find themselves in the midst of the problems between husbands and wives may need to listen and evaluate the situation with extreme care so that they do not compound an emergency by pushing it toward a separation or divorce that may not be appropriate at all.

This approach does not apply in every case of marital stress, of course, and does not warrant the revivification of an old "stick-together-at-all-costs" attitude, but its incidence is significant enough for all those who do crisis counseling to explore it as a possibility.

THE STRESS OF MARRIAGE

Five of the top ten stressors in the famous scale developed by Dr. Thomas Holmes ("The Social Readjustment Rating Scale," *Journal of Psychosomatic Research*), are related to the experience of marriage. Included are the death of a spouse as well as the experiences of divorce and separation. These are stresses that flow from the very core of the marital relationship itself, the crises that become full-blown when the strands of intimacy are broken or pulled gradually apart. Intimacy—that most sought after goal in the contemporary world—is also the source of the stress that is intrinsic to marriage.

There is enough potential for strain in any close relationship to test the adjustive capacity of the healthiest person. Suppose, however, that factors outside the relationship, not identified or perhaps not even suspected, introduce problems that may mistakenly be interpreted as indications that the marriage itself is failing. Such a condition would constitute a subtle emergency within the context of marriage that would demand careful evaluation and prudent treatment by those helpers who, as clergy or other professionals, find themselves dealing with it.

The most common example cited in the literature is that of *depression,* the effects of which are frequently misunderstood. How does this work? The symptoms of depression include increased sensitivity, a drop in sexual interest, and withdrawal from contacts with others. While this depression may have varied sources, the presence of the above signs may and often does mislead partners into thinking that they have fallen out of love.

It is not unusual for a depressed person to feel that he or she no longer loves his or her spouse. This is a result of the generally lowered emotional reactivity and does not necessarily indicate that the marriage is in trouble. The spouse, in such a situation, may experience the depressive symptoms as signals of rejection.

Such couples sometimes point to the symptoms, are puzzled by them, and actually move toward separation and divorce without understanding that the seed of the difficulty lies in the depression experienced by one of the partners. The crisis arises on a distorted premise that love has faded when, in actuality, the depressive episode, which can be treated separately from the relationship, is the basic problem.

Is There a Turning Point?

Many observers feel that in this type of marital crisis, just as in more obvious emergencies, a definite precipitant can be identified. The precipitant is that incident or point after which things seem markedly different for one or both spouses. What can this be? The parent of the husband or wife may die, thus setting off a quiet but profound reaction largely on an unconscious level. This can upset the balance of a marriage, but its source is an event outside the marital union and it must be seen in that perspective if the crisis is to be managed successfully.

A child may die, and if the resulting depression in one or both spouses is not treated, the symptoms, with blind but powerful leverage, may pull the union down upon itself. So, too, economic reverses or too many moves in too short a period to too many towns may have a negative effect on the self-esteem of one or both spouses.

Such depression can blow apart even a sturdy marriage. It causes a clear and present danger to the husband and wife, who may be able to speak about how they are not getting along and who mistakenly think that terminating the marriage is the only choice before them. As Dr. Flach has noted, "Divorce has become not only an acceptable option but, for many, a very attractive one" and persons may end a "perfectly salvageable marriage impulsively or as a way to ward off anxiety or depression not primarily rooted in marital difficulties" (p. 18).

What Can a Helper Do?

Emergency workers need to examine their own attitudes toward the solution that seems to be offered by divorce. Many have unconsciously developed a bias in favor of divorce with the notion that it is better to exercise this freedom and to start all over than it is to work patiently at discovering the sources of interpersonal conflict.

Helpers should restrain themselves from making divorce the necessary option in every case. It is odd that so many people who would feel that it was a mistake to tell others to try to make their marriages work again would not feel uneasy about encouraging at least the consideration of divorce or separation.

Counselors should take as complete a history as they can, trying, if it is possible, to discover the outlines of the classic crisis situation. If one observes a critical incident, or precipitant, after which problems began in earnest, then an investigation of the possibility of depression is in order. If, for example, the person says that "It all started after I shifted jobs," or "It hasn't been the same since I had this accident," the helper has a clear indication of the possibility that a reaction is infecting the marriage from the outside.

The next step may involve referral for treatment of the depression before effective work on the relationship in something like marriage counseling can be accomplished. The emergency here is precisely the depressed emotional reaction, which can be associated with a specific precipitant and needs treatment through referral to a competent therapist.

Closing in on this sore spot constitutes the essential crisis-counseling response. The helper need not assume responsibility for further therapy that may exceed his or her capability. Helpers need only to read the situation carefully and not make the mistake of perceiving it as a problem inherent in the marriage relationship itself.

The helper can enhance his or her own judgment about this special form of emergency by asking a simple question: What has this man or this woman lost? One can rather easily sense the echoes of a loss that has not been worked out, without having to resort to unpleasant probing.

People want to talk about what they have lost. They do it, however, in symbolic fashion, and we must be ready to catch the significance of oblique signals. This is why they develop depressions in the first place; the characteristic symptoms of depression allow them to ward off the anxiety they would have to experience if they faced the implications of their losses more directly. Moreover, this is how the symptoms get backed into the marriage, and until they are treated they will distend the marriage and make *it* appear to be the problem when it is only one of the phenomena strongly affected by the basic problem.

IDENTIFYING THE PROBLEM

Helpers are sometimes astounded at the beneficent effects that quickly follow on the identification of the problem that is intruding on the marriage relationship itself. Frequently the life of a family is pulled out of shape because its members have built their lives and their reactions around the pathology or problems of a significant member. Once that problem is remedied, the distortions can be corrected and something like happiness can return to the previously quite uncomfortable family grouping.

An example that will help counselors to understand the nature of this critical problem in marriage is that of a middle-aged businessman who has had a drinking problem for fifteen years, resulting in a stalled career, many repeated warnings from his employer and one dismissal from his job. He now seeks help out of the fear of losing his job.

What had been going on and how had it affected his marriage and his family life? The man "insisted that the only problem he had was with a boring job and that he had been mistreated by his employer ten years earlier, when he was passed over for a promotion despite the implied promise and his expectation."

Here, of course, one can note a precipitant, a turning point of sorts that was confirmed by his wife, who testified to the deteriorating nature of their marriage over the previous ten years. He had, she noted, become "increasingly bitter, irritable, and emotionally unavailable with increasing drinking." She had, in fact, come to accept her husband's early death "by withdrawing emotionally from him, finding a job as a bookkeeper, and resigning herself to the seemingly unavoidable prospect of life without him."

Obviously, this man's problems at work and his depressive reaction to being passed over for promotion had a profound and almost fatal effect on his marriage and homelife. "His depressed and self-defeating way of life over . . . ten years had been sustained by the dynamic interactions among the . . . spheres of his life. The quiet rejection by his wife . . . had played a key role in keeping him depressed."

Once the man's problem was seen in perspective it was possible to provide treatment for his depression as well as follow-up therapy for the couple, which led "to a marked improvement in marital and family relationships and a much more realistic and productive adjustment to his job." Amateur helpers encounter similar situations almost every day. If they are alert to the crisis nature of the intrusive elements, they can make much better and more effective recommendations and referrals.

What Are You Liable to Find?

Helpers who become involved in working with marriages that are under stress may also discover other factors that both cause and aggravate the crisis. Since the range of possible problems is very broad, counselors need a sense of realism to inform the judgments they make about the salvageability of some relationships. That many people break up over problems that they could work through is undoubtedly true, but if there are signs of other, deeper human problems, the helper should stand back and not force assistance on a situation that may be analogous to an inoperable physical condition.

Thus, for example, if counselors discover a significant degree of chronic mental illness in one of the partners, if, for example, husband or wife is clearly psychotic or suffering from some personality disorder, the referral for the treatment of the individual takes precedence over all other potential moves.

When you go inside a person's house, you form a very different picture of him or her from the one you formed when seeing him or her only in social settings. So, too, helpers get a good view of the inside of a marriage, and this is sometimes as bizarre or as barren as the couple's house. People can and do marry for severely neurotic reasons, and rounds of stressful interaction, like those in a prizefight, may not only signify their psychological problems but actually provide the means through which they adjust to each other.

Craziness incarnate is what helpers come upon, and their ability to intervene successfully is severely limited. Doing something may just disturb a relationship that, though quite bizarre, has achieved some equilibrium.

So, too, the discovery that some serious problem, such as drug addiction, lies at the heart of the marital stress, dictates treatment of this concern rather than focusing on the marriage itself. Naturally, helpers who care about others want to be positive and optimistic, especially since there are marriages that can successfully survive what seem to be serious and possibly terminal crises. Such an outlook is commendable, but it must always be tested against the hard cutting-edge of the incredibly varied possibilities of human beings.

Two Cautions

Few advances in medicine have received as much publicity as the treatment of manic-depressive disease by use of lithium carbonate. Popular literature makes the chemical solution to depressive problems seem immediately or imminently available for everyone. Maturity and professional caution make most experts far more qualified in their judgments of the applicability of such treatments.

Emergency helpers should not think that there is a magic cure or a special pill that will lift away the depression described in this chapter. Depression is an exceedingly complicated phenomenon, and its proper diagnosis and treatment should be left to experts. Helpers can identify the gross signs of depression, especially in marriage partners, but they must never promise too much in terms of chemical treatment based merely on the spate of articles or such medications. This is the time for them to make a sensible referral.

Counselors should also be prepared for a phenomenon that is quite commonly observed. Intrude in any marriage, even for healthy purposes, and you may disrupt a balance that cannot easily be regained. This is also true in situations in which one of the partners may be receiving treatment for some problem that is specifically his or hers. If one spouse begins to get better, that may cause the other spouse to get worse.

Getting along badly may be something a married couple is strangely accustomed to, and any change in one may cause a compensatory reaction in the other. There is the course of reactivity in any close relationship, and helpers should not panic if this seems to happen. They need to deal with it as part of the dynamic progression that issues from any crisis that is in the process of resolution.

For Further Reading

Flach, Frederic, "Marriage: New Therapeutic Dimensions," *Psychiatric Annals* 7:6 (June 1979), p. 14.

Grunebaum, H., and Christ, J. (eds.) *Contemporary Marriage: Structure, Dynamics, and Therapy.* Boston: Little, Brown & Co., 1967.

Gurman, A. S., and Rice, D. G. (eds.) *Couples in Conflict.* New York: Jason Aronson, 1975.

Holmes, Thomas, "The Social Readjustment Rating Scale," *Journal of Psychosomatic Research* 2 (1967) p. 213.

Sager, C. J. "The Treatment of Married Couples." In *American Handbook of Psychiatry,* vol. 3, S. Arieti et al. (eds.). New York: Basic Books, 1974, pp. 213–24.

Smith, R., and Alexander, A. *Counseling Couples in Groups.* Springfield, Ill.: Charles C. Thomas, 1974.

Yalom, I. *The Theory and Practice of Group Psychotherapy.* New York: Basic Books, 1970.

SEVENTEEN

Crises for the Helper

PEOPLE who feel the pressure of duty seldom want to turn down a request for assistance. Neither do they wish to make a referral for too little reason. So, too, helpers who are highly motivated and who like other people do not excuse themselves easily from the demands of their work. Even though they may theoretically recognize that their burdens are excessive, they can find reasons to continue to bear them without taking a break; they feel, they say, well enough to carry on even when others tell them that they are working too hard. Indeed, this is a widespread syndrome—the exhausted helper with no convenient or permitted opportunity to seek refreshment.

Counselors are keenly aware of the damage that can occur when certain professionals keep at their tasks too long and too intensely. Everyone knows about the stress that is the occupational hazard of the air-traffic controller. During the coming decade we will hear more and more about the general problem of "burn-out," the headline-style word that describes a variety of complaints and conflicts that are associated with excessive exposure to highly demanding occupational conditions. At times this is aggravated by an overinvestment of the helper in the work at hand.

Obviously, such a condition can easily arise for persons who find themselves working with crises on a continuing basis. Such may, in fact, be the type of counseling that nonprofessional counselors are asked to do more than any other. They do not, after all, work on an extended basis with the troubled persons who seek their assistance. They do not carry case-loads the way trained professionals do.

But nonprofessional counselors do get a call when some emergency arises or when something out of the usual occurs in the office, the school, or the neighborhood. It would not be unusual for those working in religious ministry to face everything from wife-beating and attempted suicide to drug abuse and bereavement within the course of one twenty-four hour period. They are continuously asked to insert themselves into crisis situation in which their involvement may be crucial and intense— and yet quite brief.

This is the nature of their work, and while this relieves them of the obligations of longer-term relationships, it also imposes on them the penalties that are attached to relationships that are always breaking off just when the prospect of progress is emerging. There is enormous stress associated with exposure to the worst of human reactions without the antidote of improvement.

It may be fair to state that some nonprofessional counselors live emergency-oriented lives, that they are always poised on the rim of disaster and, in fact, their work itself constitutes an extended crisis. Helpers need to learn to appraise the stress of their work and to identify the dangerous overloads that may take this sort of toll on them unless they learn to manage them more effectively.

It is often difficult for persons with a sincere desire to help to admit that they have taken on too much or that they have seriously compromised their own effectiveness by failing to temper their demanding schedules with periods of change or rest. "Burn-out" is an ugly word for an ugly condition, and, sadly enough, overworked helpers frequently discover that there is nobody around to offer them assistance when, heading toward burn-out, they are in need of it.

More often than not, another crisis arises at just the moment when they feel like discussing their own stress, and something else is asked of them. It is routine for this to happen and should be accepted as the first law of helping: When the helpers want help, they are asked to give it instead.

SIGNS AND SYMPTOMS

Perhaps the second law of emergency counselors should read: There is no shortage of trouble. It follows that helpers should not expect that things will ever slow down. They will, in fact, pick up, so that the helper's opportunities for change or for rest will become fewer and fewer. This is compounded for helpers who are good at assisting others, for their reputation spreads rapidly.

Wise helpers, whether they are lawyers, teachers, or ministers, must accept the truth that the world will not slow down or change its pace for them. Natural breaks will not be delivered to them, so they have to make their own.

This is a difficult truth for many of them to accept, especially if they have a streak of the "savior" complex running through their souls. The reward of helping is legitimate and should not be denied to anyone. The need to help may, however, be exaggerated, so that it becomes almost neurotic in form. Crisis work is no place for individuals who suffer from "rescue fantasies" or for those who feel that they must redeem or change the entire world. Ideologues may become overwhelmed in their helping activities by the tension of trying both to help and to evangelize at the same time.

Helping is a fundamental human activity, and the motivations involved in it are usually mixed. Counselors should learn to understand and accept the various strands of their motivations so that they can take their effects into account during their work. They need, in other words, to learn to observe themselves with understanding, so that they can use their strengths well and avoid the overextension that has led so many people to burn-out in one form or another.

Watching themselves and their own needs, helpers can do something about themselves when it becomes impossible for them to do anything about the enormous and constant difficulties in the world around them. Counselors need a philosophy of life as well as a noncondemnatory appreciation of their own personal psychology.

When counselors discover, for example, that they cannot leave their crisis work behind, that they cannot let the person or persons go onto the next stage of recovery, they are experiencing some aspect of the killing stress of their work.

When counselors find that their own personal lives are shrinking and that they have no time for the ordinary kinds of recreation they would recommend to others, they have good evidence that they are overworked.

When counselors have difficulty in concentrating on other tasks, or when they feel anxiety developing over unresolved conflicts of their own, they should recognize that it is time to take measures to help themselves before they attempt to continue to assist others.

The possible symptoms are many, but all point to a steady diet of intense work that has gradually taken its toll. Identification of any more than casual distress—that is, of a burgeoning and disruptive problem that is out of the ordinary—should alert them to seek assistance for themselves.

Emergency workers have been known to suffer from "contagious exhaustion'' after too much exposure to the emotional reactions that are typical of people who are working through a life crisis. One can absorb only so much ambivalence and can feel the pull of only so much irrational expectation before the stress asserts itself. People in an emergency may demand that we support them, that we accept their devouring dependency of their never-ending desire for reassurance: these are the daily fare of crisis workers. But these can be very wearing, and helpers must take the time to examine their own reactions in order, without guilt, to monitor the level of stress and keep it from becoming excessive.

SOME SPECIAL CASES

Burn-out becomes a proximate difficulty for those who must wrestle each day with persons who are in the throes of making moral decisions that have far-reaching consequences in their lives. It is difficult to work as a counselor with those planning a family or those contemplating steps such as abortion about which the counselor may have firm personal convictions. The added stress of trying to help when one feels that the other is making a self-destructive decision (e.g., about drug use) is also enormous.

The very fact that helpers possess certain values subjects them to an added source of stress when they are working with those who do not understand or who wish to reject such values. This is a widespread difficulty about which little is said. Counselors do not abandon their own convictions even when they try not to force them on others. They must understand that certain problems will arise that will cause them to feel an internal conflict that is merely a by-product of the crisis with which they are dealing.

While counselors may have to withhold moral judgments in order to help others through the emotional aspects of the crisis, they are not freed from the stress that such a balancing act may demand of them. This is particularly true for the clergy, who may have to restrain their moralizing at certain stages of the crises with which they deal. Nothing is more wearing than trying to help a world that seems—and *seems* is important—to have flouted the standards that the helper prizes.

WHAT CAN HELPERS DO?

There is no insurance against the emotional damage that can occur as a side effect in crisis work. The only one who can prepare and manage the emergencies that must be dealt with in a manner that will maximize assistance to the other while minimizing stress to the self is the helper.

Perhaps the first step in responding therapeutically to the self is by systematic listening to one's own emotional reactions. These are filled with information about both ourselves, those we work with, and the delicate interaction that is our constantly shifting relationship with them.

Our feelings are the compass on which we can read the "true north" of the direction in which we are heading. An alertness to them and a readiness to interpret them accurately is the best way to keep ourselves in a healthy emotional condition. Otherwise we will be pulled along by them, and we will not understand why we are reacting in certain ways or why we are so confused or in conflict about certain aspects of our work. If a nonprofessional discovers that emergency work has become a major part of the week's activities, listening to his or her emotions is indispensable to survival.

If helpers find it difficult to sort out their own feelings, they should seek out someone who can help them to do it. That might be a professional counselor who would be willing to supervise their work for a certain fee or, failing that, a skilled associate or group of colleagues who may be able to come together for this specific purpose.

Secondly, helpers should schedule their work in such a way that they do not unnecessarily pile up situations that are emotionally draining on the same day. Many nonprofessional counselors, especially those in religious ministry, cannot very easily schedule the emergencies with which they will deal. However, they can, except in unusual circumstances such as a disaster, order their work so that it does not overextend them on any given day. They can anticipate, based on experience, that, for example, hospital visits or other specific activities will exact a certain amount of spiritual and emotional effort from them. It may not be wise to arrange marriage-counseling sessions on the evening of the same day when the person knows he or she will already be under stress.

There is little that can be done for the emergency-lovers who throw themselves into one crisis after another with the passion of the lawyers who are ambulance-chasers. When helpers find that they cannot live without the incidental excitement of a crisis in their lives, when they love emergencies the way General Patton is reputed to have loved war, they are in trouble and need to pause for serious self-examination.

Just as in emergencies there is no substitute for common sense, so there is no substitute for it in emergency workers either. They are facing a symptom more than an ideal when they feel that people cannot get along without them. It is to just such signs that weary helpers should pay heed if they seriously want to preserve their best selves for their work with others.

Learning about community resources and employing them without hesitation at the time of emergencies is also a very practical way to insure good mental health for the helper. Even the smallest community possesses certain resources, or has access to them in nearby communities, that can relieve helpers of thinking that everything depends on them. Learning the networks that have already been developed can redeem the helper from the feeling of isolation that descends when he or she lacks proper information about community reserves and referrals.

Continuing education is also a great help to the nonprofessional counselor, even if this is achieved only through reading or through attending occasional seminars or lectures. Such activity increases self-confidence, while it also expands the helper's store of practical information about dealing with crises.

An Example: Breaking Bad News

There are many varieties of bad news: death, injury, dismissal, scholastic failure, the thousand small disappointments that only the affected person can appreciate, as well as major problems involving scandal or crime. Each one of these is almost certainly related to a crisis in somebody else's life. Indeed, the person charged with facing another individual with a revelation that the other may not suspect to be public knowledge—for example, confronting a colleague about excessive drinking or the report of unethical or immoral behavior—may be the agent of the actual onset of crisis. The breaker of bad news may be the proximate precipitant of a problem that has been building up for a long time. Almost everyone who has the instincts to help has been asked at some point to carry out the unpleasant task of informing another person of one kind of bad news or another.

This is also a stressful moment for the one charged with carrying out the task. The minister who is always the one elected to tell the wife that her husband has had a fatal accident, the police official who bears bad tidings to the family of a patrolman injured on duty, the principal who must discuss reports of child-molesting with a previously trusted member of the faculty: These people are on the front lines of a hazardous activity. If their commitment is to the individual rather than to just breaking the news, then they cannot, like a newspaper plopped at the door, merely break the bad news in a dramatic and unfeeling way. They have to help the person over the first stage of the crisis; they have to help the individual sustain the impact of the blow and work through the predictable reactions of shame or grief. They may have to arrange for some follow-through as well.

It is not surprising that some professionals have adopted what has, ironically enough, become known as a "professional" attitude in breaking bad news. This means that they maintain distance and an impersonal manner in order to shield themselves from the stings of repeated emotional involvements that are difficult to manage. Thus, some informants favor an almost brutal approach. They feel that the other has to know and that one might as well get it all out as fast and as clearly as possible. Managing the effects becomes the business of somebody else. One may be able to understand, if not exactly condone, such an approach.

However, there must be a middle-ground, especially for those professionals such as the clergy whose calling demands that they minister through the impact stage of the bad news and that they stay with the bereaved or the indicted during the period of reaction. It is not a compromise to accept the middle-ground position; rather, it is a sound option, both for the good of the other and for the emotional stability of the helper. What can the helper do to prepare for such difficult but not uncommon assignments?

PRACTICAL STEPS

First of all, the helper should make sure that he or she is in full possession of accurate information about the relevant incident and any circumstances or other facts connected with it. This is particularly true when the occasion for breaking bad news has to do with the revelation of previously masked behavior, as in confronting a colleague about breaches of ethics. Perhaps there is no situation that escalates more swiftly than that crisis in which a person is accused of misbehaving. Frequently the evidence is sketchy and circumstantial, but even when the facts are indisputable, the tendency to dramatize and overreact is commonplace. In fact, the course that is often followed is to bring the information to the highest authority in the organization or social system before it is discussed with the individual.

When this occurs, the relayers of the information have placed the bad news in the hands of someone who must, by virtue of official responsibility, do something about it. That may preclude the constructive intervention that can take place when the initial facing of the problem is at a lower level of authority.

A plan of carrying out the breaking of bad news should focus on the lowest rung in the ladder of escalation. This is not to minimize the difficulty—for other steps can be taken easily if the need arises—but to maximize the possibility of helping the other person to get assistance freely and adequately before the matter demands authoritative action. This is not to play down the problem; it is to humanize the approach to it and to exhaust all lower levels of managing the critical phases of such incidents before automatically making it a subject for disciplinary action.

The helper should not only plan the steps of the confrontation but also rehearse mentally and emotionally the likely reactions to this procedure. Such anticipation of what is likely to happen enables the helper to maintain a personal interest without being swept away by unexpected anger, denial, or other reaction. Experience teaches a great deal about this, but if one cannot anticipate the reactions of the other, one can at least have some idea of one's own. Even this limited knowledge is of great use for the helper.

Have a plan for follow-up assistance. This may come through referral to psychiatric or other assistance or through an orchestration of community resources and helpers from other professions—social workers, clergy, special teachers, home visiting nurses—to continue to assist the person or social system that is strained by the bad news.

Common sense dictates these simple steps as the soundest way to manage the stress of the helping person. There will be enough stress anyway, so whatever steps can be taken in advance to handle it constructively should be taken. Flying blind, relying on a Micawber's conviction that "everything will work out," only builds tension and leads to the symptoms of burn-out that were described earlier.

EIGHTEEN

Crises of Separation and Divorce

No clergyperson, lawyer, or teacher needs to be alerted to the possibility of involvement, at some stage or other, in what we may consider the unfolding crises of divorce and separation. Whether they like it or not, such professionals find that they are often on the periphery, and frequently in the very midst, of such problems.

There has also been a torrent of literature and opinion on the subject of marriage and divorce in recent years. As we observed earlier, the breakup of a marriage has become almost a fashionable cultural set-piece. Helpers may find themselves in crisis, that is, in conflict about whether their task is to facilitate what some claim can be "creative divorce" or whether, particularly if their main professional identification is the clergy, they must help hold the line against those forces that would challenge or disrupt the stability of family life.

Before examining some of the facts and issues related to separation and divorce, therefore, it is important for nonprofessional counselors to understand their own position in the welling tide of circumstances that laps at the edge of their daily work. There is no question that the work of the counselor called in at a specific point of crisis in a marriage can be profoundly affected—and sometimes seriously compromised—by the prevailing mood or opinion both of culture in general and of some specific subset thereof, as, for example, in the helper's own religious or ethnic tradition. What are some of these changing cultural attitudes and how may they affect the work of the counselor?

DIVORCE/PRO

The acceptance of divorce as a solution to a life problem or as the natural resolution of a marriage relationship has, of course, found numerous supporters in the last several decades. Even formerly staunch defenders of the marital bond, such as some of the strong church groups, have modified their positions and, in a variety of ways, have come to terms with the reality of divorce and the impossibility of preserving every marriage relationship.

This has been accomplished partially through the integration of modern psychological insights, and the more subtle understanding of human motivation that they generate, into the day-to-day dealing with marriage of such groups. It has also been aided by an extension of principles and legal processes that have always been present within certain traditions, including the Roman Catholic, that have recognized the complexity of personal motivation and the conditions that, in fact, suggest that some people may not really be able to come together in marriage.

The climate has definitely become one in which the crisis-intervenor, even if a religious figure, does not necessarily feel that the marriage has to be preserved at all costs. Indeed, many clergy have full-time ministries in counseling the divorced who wish the understanding and support of their church groups. Hard as it may seem to accept, many have looked deeply at the actual marriage relationships with which they have worked and have wondered, as writers and artists have, just how many fully contracted marriages do exist. They have also become wiser about the complex of factors and other relationships that maintain the stability of some marriages. There has been a blossoming awareness that very little is clear and simple about human relationships and that some haze of ambivalence trails off even the best of them.

Such a state naturally influences counselors in their interpretations of the critical events in the marriages about which they are consulted. It makes them more tolerant, both of human frailty and of divorce or separation as a means of handling problems. Indeed, some counselors, as previously discussed, have taken on the mantle of advocacy and may not have examined their own feelings or convictions in some time.

DIVORCE/CON

As the last generation of this century dawns, there are signs of at least a halting reappraisal of the use of separation and divorce as solutions to relationship difficulties. While one may anticipate a certain cyclical quality to attitudes toward our institutions, it is not easy to define this shift or to predict its possible long-term effects.

It is difficult to define because a wish to stabilize the churning contemporary environment may be a deep and broadly shared need at this time.

When old values seem not to hold at all, there is a societal urge to restructure these and to return to them because of their reassuring qualities. People need anchors and foundations. Thus, the restatement of traditional Roman Catholic teachings about sex and marriage by Pope John Paul II not only aims at delineating traditional teachings but also at binding society itself together around the marriage and family unit.

Disenchantment with the romantic ideal is not yet a large factor in American culture, but there are those who are beginning to wonder if the chaos that may follow the attempt to gratify every romantic wish does not make this imperative. Some have begun to wonder whether the marriage ideal based on free choice has worked any better than that based on arranged unions. This is the natural consequence of extended exposure to ambivalence and uncertainty; it contributes in a small but significant way to the reappraisal of divorce and separation that is going on in our society.

Nor should anyone undervalue the impact of a renewed emphasis on the family as the basic and irreplaceable agency of both continuity and human communion. Even pragmatically, for fear of the fragmentation of society that might otherwise result, there is a new emphasis on the family as a unique source of identity and fulfillment. The forces that will emphasize this over the next decade are just now forming, but their influence is bound to be great. One can already see a prophecy of this in the arts—in contemporary plays, for example—and it is important for helpers to be able to read such signs of the times.

A new respect for old positions does not necessarily represent woolyheaded regression, but one would be naïve not to expect that fundamentalist forces would express themselves very strongly on the issues of marriage and divorce. Perhaps one of the clearest targets of criticism by such groups will be the notion of counseling or therapy itself. A distrust of psychology has already developed, if only because, like all others, it is an imperfect human science. A deeper attack, however, has been initiated by some, who regard psychological counseling, unless distinctively Christian, as an enemy of the stability of marriage.

Most of this criticism is aimed at humanistic psychology, at those schools of counseling based loosely on "self" theory, such as the work of Carl Rogers, and while the attacks are frequently overgeneralized and inaccurate, they represent not only a return to what seem to be more simple verities but also another example of a growing distate for or weariness with psychological techniques that seem to ignore the need for hardship and sacrifice in life.

One can also anticipate a growing disillusionment on the part of many people with the oversold virtues of various forms of "liberation." The right or wrong of these is not the issue: The fact is that many people do not feel freer, but more bound by the circumstances of their lives. This painful situation will move many to react against causes that were extremely popular over the last generation and, as an incidental effect, will bring about a readiness to deal with marriage as something with deeper roots and more abiding demands—and, consequently, greater satisfactions—than it has been accorded in recent times.

HELPERS THEMSELVES

No professional, whatever the field, can appraise the crises of marriage without some awareness of the factors that are steadily working and reworking our feelings and opinions. Before helpers join themselves to the work of crisis intervention in marriage, they need some cultural understanding as well as some examination of their own attitudes.

Have counselors become advocates, even subtly, one way or the other in regard to separation and divorce? Have they accepted, because of personal experience or popular pressure, a set of opinions that they have not subjected to analysis lately? Do they have the patience to maintain a broad view while they are pressed urgently against the critical incident of separation or divorce? Have they allowed themselves, unwittingly, to become part of a procedure in which the individual, without any free choice or personal motivation, must seek their help to fulfill the legal requirements of certain states (e.g., mandatory reconciliation counseling)?

Does the helper have some understanding of the meanings of transference and countertransference and the role these may play in the emotionally charged atmosphere of the critical incidents of marriage dissolution? Is the helper aware of the other community resources that may have to be called on in order to truly be of assistance to persons who are seeking assistance?

Obviously, counselors need not engage in masochistic self-examination before they intervene in the extremely stressful emergencies of human relationships, but they need a cultural and personal grounding that allows them the perspective that is so necessary for effective counseling. This way of looking at things enables them to maintain self-possession, which is such a key element in any crisis counselor, as well as a realistic sense of what is going on without allowing it to become unnecessarily distorted.

What Is Going On?

America's bicentennial year witnessed more than three million persons involved directly in the dissolution of a marriage: There were approximately a million divorces, with an average of almost two children per divorce. This means that one and one-half percent of the entire population were directly affected by divorce. The compounded and impacted stress represented by such figures might make the heartiest counselors cringe, as they realize the number of critical events and experiences, each of them wrenching and painful, associated with divorce, both before and after the event itself. Helpers would have no lack of work even if they confined their attention solely to marital emergencies.

Other evidence suggests the slowly unfolding nature of these emergencies. The children of divorced or separated parents seem to have a statistically higher probability of recreating this experience in their own lives. There is, then, a generational character to the problems of marriage and divorce; the emergencies string out for years, like land mines sewn across the still-shaded future. The emergency worker may find that he or she is involved at any time in this long, sad continuum.

Side Effects

Physicians must be particularly sensitive to the correlates of these emergencies. Sometimes the pain is expressed in the language of greater vulnerability to illness. There are data to suggest that those who have been involved in separation or divorce may have a greater susceptibility to medical illness, motor vehicle accident mortality, psychiatric hospitalization, and suicide and homicide. In other words, such experiences are, according to demographic data, more likely to happen to divorced people than to single, widowed or married people of the same age, sex, race, or social class.

The period of postdivorce adjustment is also hazardous. This can be an especially difficult time for those who are older at the time of divorce, those who have been married longer, and those who have just recently been divorced. Emergency psychological problems are also a greater possibility for those who receive a divorce at the suggestion of a spouse, those who had previously encountered opposition to the marriage, and those with inadequate economic status. When generally difficult conditions in a country, such as a recession, tighten the grip of stress a little bit further, then the possibility of further crises is sharply increased.

Main Source of Stress

In an attempt to deal with the varied nature of the events surrounding the crisis of divorce, Bohannan (*Divorce and After*) has enumerated six different types of *loss* that accompany this event. Legal divorce is only one of these, and, from the viewpoint of the counselor, may only give rise to new opportunities for marriage.

The other faces of separation must also be understood if one is to become involved in assisting the individual going through this crisis period. These include *emotional divorce,* the result of the loss of the loved one; *economic divorce,* through which property that has been shared in common must be divided; *co-parental divorce,* which centers on custody and visitation rights for the children; *community divorce,* which involves the attitudes and changing relationships with relatives and friends; and, by no means least, *psychic divorce,* or the process of being born again as a separate and autonomous individual.

These may appear as relatively independent sources of assault on the individual's ability to maintain a healthy personal adjustment, and, like silent invaders, may infiltrate the marriage relationship long before the actual divorce. Their effects may also linger long after the divorce is actually achieved. As some students of these events have put it, "divorce is but one stage in the process of marital disintegration and personal readjustment" (Bloom, Asher, and White, "Marital Disruption as a Stressor," *Psychological Bulletin*).

Loss is at the core of many of the crises that begin before divorce and continue afterward. Some appreciation of loss and its effects, especially depression, and of the need to properly mourn these changes is essential to helpers who intervene anywhere along the path.

Bloom, Asher, and White have also identified a significant complex of problems that arise for persons going through marital disruption. These include: weakened social support systems and the need for time and a place to work through a variety of feelings, including the anxiety, depression, and hostility, that follow upon the various losses. Such persons also pass through crises that center on learning the details of child rearing and learning a new social role as a single or divorced person or as a single parent.

Sharp crises can also be associated with utterly practical challenges, such as managing finances, planning for education and future employ-

ment, and developing an understanding of one's legal rights and obligations. These may grow into serious, quasiemergency states at the time of
separation itself.

CENTRAL PROCESS: MOURNING

As mentioned before, loss and the need to mourn are intrinsically
related to these events. Such losses can only be processed by mourning,
and helpers must understand both this truth and some of the dynamics of
mourning if they are to be truly effective in assisting those ravaged by the
experience of marital disruption. Indeed, the way in which a person
faces and weathers the multiple crises associated with marital separation
may depend on his or her capacity to mourn and to acquire the skills,
social and other, that are necessary for life to continue.

One of the problems for all persons is that they often learn ways to
respond to difficult situations that are essentially unproductive. These
are termed "maladaptive responses" and may be observed in the person
who, for example, withdraws at the first sign of conflict, or uses other
unhelpful mechanisms, such as drinking, isolation, or some repetitive
pattern of unsuccessful argumentation, whenever marital adjustment is
threatened. These poor solutions are, in a way, signs of a relationship
that is accumulating difficulties the way scar tissue is a sign of a stressed
heart.

In a family, one can frequently observe that certain defective patterns
are repeated until they become strongly fixed. They are, in fact, poor
ways of dealing with losses that have been occurring on a real or imagined level during the course of the relationship. Later on, minor issues
can trigger these maladaptive responses, as well as associated feelings of
anger, grief, guilt, and bitterness that were caused by the losses earlier,
unidentified. The complaints, and the almost unapproachable negative
feelings that the counselor faces when a crisis erupts, have their origins
in past aspects of the relationship. No helper can expect to heal or
transform these long-smoldering emotions successfully without a sense
of where they came from and of how deeply they may be established.

In the next chapter we will discuss some of the specific counseling
concepts connected with the crises of separation and divorce.

For Further Reading

Blechman, E. A., & Manning, M. "A Reward-Cost Analysis of the Single-
Parent Family." In *Behavior Modification and Families* (Eric J. Mash, L. A.
Hammerlynck, and L. C. Handy, eds.). New York: Brunner/Mazel, 1976.

Bohannan, P. (ed.) *Divorce and After*. Garden City, New York: Doubleday, 1970.

Bloom, B. L., Ashcr, S. J.& White, S. W. "Marital Disruption as a Stressor," *Psychological Bulletin 85,* (1978), pp. 867–94.

Brown, E. M. "Divorce Counseling." In *Treating Relationships* (David H. L. Olson, ed.). Lake Mills, Iowa: Graphic Publishing Co., Inc., 1976.

Jacobson, N. S., & Margolin, G. *Marital Therapy: Strategies Based on Social Learning and Behavior Exchange Principles*. New York: Brunner/Mazel, 1979.

Johnson, S. M. *First Person Singular: Living The Good Life Alone*. New York: Lippincott, 1977.

Kressell, K., & Deustch, M. "Divorce Therapy: An In-Depth Survey of Therapist's Views," *Family Process 16,* (1977), pp. 413–44.

Paul, N. L. "The Role of Mourning and Empathy in Conjoint Marital Ther.py," In *Family Therapy and Disturbed Families* (G. Zuk, and I. Boszormenyi-Nagy, eds.). Palo Alto, Cal.: Science and Behavior Books, 1967 (sixth printing, 1975).

Tooley, K. M. "'Irreconcilable Differences' Between Parent and Child: A Case Report of Interactional Pathology," *American Journal of Orthopsychiatry* 48 (1978), pp. 703–16.

NINETEEN

Crises by Phone

THE telephone has, in its myriad incarnations, become an indispensable part of life; its presence is ubiquitous but accepted as a constant rather than a miraculous variable in the human situation. Some researchers have speculated about whether talking on the telephone changes a person's personality, and ordinary people sometimes observe that they can say things on the phone that they cannot say in person while others discover that a substantial part of their relationship with others is maintained through the use of this remarkable instrument.

It is no surprise that the telephone, symbol of a new age, should have become a means of dealing with the troubled and that an entire specialty of crisis assistance has developed around it under various titles and for highly specialized purposes. Thus there are "hot lines" for suicide prevention and various other specific problems, including the Christmas holiday blues. We also know, of course, that the telephone is the medium used by certain troubled persons to express their emotional difficulties, as, for example, with obscene callers.

The telephone is part of the equipment of practicing professionals who understand that "being on call" may literally refer to accepting or returning calls to patients or clients who are in distress. It is no less true for the nonprofessional counselor who, even without "on call" responsibilities, finds that he or she is in an equivalent position many times every week. In fact, the lawyer, the minister, and others who deal with the needy public may find that many of the crises with which they deal come to them through, or may demand the extensive use of, the telephone. Understanding some of the special characteristics of the telephone is a necessary step for all those who must use it to deal with emergencies.

CHARACTERISTICS OF THE PHONE

Psychiatrist Warren B. Miller has written what might be considered the definitive essay on the properties of the telephone ("The Telephone in Out-patient Psychotherapy," *American Journal of Psychotherapy*). Among the features the telephone possesses that affect the quality of communication on it is its power to reduce the distance separating its users. While this is obvious and, indeed, the very purpose for its invention, we may not reflect on the more subtle aspects of this capacity to overcome the barrier of spatial separation.

The telephone uniquely joins the experiences of distance and intimacy, so that helpers can find themselves involved instantly in emergencies that are taking place outside the normal setting of their work with others. A helper can easily be drawn into things at a distance precisely because of the nature of the telephone; this automatically introduces a number of logistic and psychological complications.

For example, any person who uses the phone persistently can reach another person, even a stranger, or, in our concern, a helper who may have had no previous relationship with the caller. Indeed, the helper may not even know the person seeking assistance. This is one of the problems intrinsic to persons who are, in a sense, public helpers, like members of the clergy. They can be sought out, for a variety of reasons, by those who, except for their voices and their stories, are total strangers to them. In a world in which many persons carry "beepers" in order to keep in touch with emergency and other calls, the role of the phone in crisis work is obviously large and complicated.

Because of these circumstances it is easy to understand why the temporal distortions introduced by the telephone must be taken into account by helpers. The phone, useful and indispensable as it is in crisis work, also breaks the generally accepted groundrules of helping. It cuts across the requirements of a certain setting and a specified time; of course, this is why the telephone is such a powerful instrument at the time of a crisis.

Accepting all that, however, counselors should be aware that some persons, even in crises, may, consciously or otherwise, use the phone because it shifts the center of control toward them. They can call when they wish, they can prolong the discussion, or interrupt it, all the time heightening the gradient of anxiety that rises in every crisis situation. Some professional helpers find that they spend so much time dealing with patients by phone outside of regular office hours that they charge for these consultations. They professionalize these phone consultations in an unambiguous manner, a strategy that is unavailable to the counselor

whose main identification is with some profession other than psycho-therapy. Perhaps it is enough to observe that the properties of the phone that we take for granted—that it transcends time and space—are variables helpers must examine carefully for their possible implication in emergency work with others.

What Dr. Miller terms the "single channel" nature of telephonic communication—that it is limited to vocal cues only—is one of the reasons that makes this different from ordinary conversation and heightens the possibilities of transference and countertransference complications. When the other person hears only the voice of the emergency worker, he or she may be much freer to project unconscious feelings onto this vague screen. Indeed, the featureless nature of the helper will increase this tendency (which may, in reverse, also generate countertransference reactions in the helper) and counselors must, therefore, be extremely alert to this possibility.

While it is a fundamental of crisis counseling that helpers can tolerate the other's pushing of their dependent needs more than in ordinary therapy, the counselor must still be able to distinguish these different kinds of psychological phenomena in order to read the situation as clearly as possible. The telephone, in other words, maximizes the chances that transference feelings, positive or negative, may be operating. This may be particularly true if the phone calls seem timed to interfere with the helper's life, that is, if they come late at night, only when he or she is eating or preparing to go out, etc.

The manipulative possibilities of the telephone are enormous; this is one of the reasons it is used to sell merchandise to people in their homes. The helper must monitor this, not to become paranoid about every call, but to appreciate the fact that more is involved than the mere communication of facts about a crisis. The person on the other end of the phone is always revealing something of his or her true self and style with others.

How Is This Person Using the Phone?

That may well be a sensible question for helpers, even as they are jotting down the details of an emergency that are being told to them. The fact is that with strangers we can never be quite sure how they are using the phone or exactly what all the subtleties of the communication may be. Oftentimes, the call is straightforward, and although the situation has the characteristics of a crisis, the caller can cope very well with some reassurance and direction about what concrete steps should be taken.

Many of us need reassurance from time to time when we are facing minor crises. Much of the telephone work done by nonprofessional counselors consists in offering encouragement in this manner. Indeed, the clergy may find that much of their ministry to the downhearted can be carried out quite effectively by phone. It is, therefore, an excellent medium for follow-up after a serious crisis, during that period of readjustment and reintegration into life that follows the resolution of the initial disruption.

On the other hand, we must admit that the phone, familiar object that it is, is also a mystery. We are not sure of just how people use it, of what gratifications it may deliver to them. Dependent and independent persons use it differently; those who are plagued with ambivalent feelings may employ it to express these feelings, because it permits closeness and distance, and the tension between them, at the same time.

Helpers may need some self-examination about their own use of the phone. Just as the hostile may use the phone against others or in order to manipulate them, so too may helpers take refuge behind the phone, enhancing their own sense of power and control or saving themselves from closer involvement in difficult emotional situations. The telephone is used almost without thinking in our culture; emergency workers cannot afford to ignore the many meanings it can have in their work.

Practical Considerations

What does the counselor need to accomplish after receiving an emergency call? This is an important agenda to pursue if only to reduce the anxiety that the nonprofessional may experience when such a call comes through. Getting their own feelings under control is a major objective for helpers in dealing with crises by telephone.

To this end, counselors need to make some evaluation about the severity of the crisis. As Gene Brockopp has observed ("Crisis Intervention: Theory, Process and Practice," *Counseling by Telephone*), an important preliminary question is "How much time do I have before I must make a decision regarding this person?" Most crises do not involve life or death, and the establishment of a sensible time perspective can remove much of the tension that the counselor would otherwise experience.

Next, the counselor must set to work right from the beginning of the relationship, even if the caller is someone already known. The helper can do this by quickly "tuning in" to the feelings of the other person, by demonstrating, through responses, that what the caller is describing and feeling is understood. This is not the time for extensive therapeutic exploration, but good responses build the essential foundations of trust upon which further help must rest.

It is never wise to employ any tricks to develop trust; that is the equivalent of manipulation and can hardly ever be considered therapeutic. Trust is a function of our capacity to be ourselves without ulterior motives in relationship to others, and helpers who are not dissemblers will project trustworthiness without effort. The simple effort to be understanding augments this very well and should, in most cases, be sufficient to establish confidence with a caller.

At times counselors will talk to persons who are deeply conflicted about trusting anybody; one cannot convince them through rational argument or promises, particularly when their very problem centers on their own difficulty with entrusting themselves to others. Helpers need not feel that they fail in such telephonic meetings; they do, on the other hand, learn something of the severity of the other person's emotional problems that helps them form a working diagnosis of the situation.

Those who wish to help should make an early effort to get to the specific core of the emergency. Is it an ongoing incident in which some intervention must be made? Is it a problem with a history that sheds light on its present manifestation? Is it some other person? What, in other words, is the essence of the crisis? The emergency helper should get to the point, so that some judgment can be made about the steps that need to be taken. Getting the point is essential in order to head in the right direction.

Naturally, the helper must make an early judgment on the suicide potential in the situation. If there is a clear and present danger, and if the caller admits to having a plan, the helper must be prepared to act without delay to contact relatives and arrange for treatment and possible hospitalization.

The action may well depend on an assessment and mobilization of the patient's strengths and available resources. The caller, caught up in the problem, may well neglect to identify the resources at hand. These may reside in the individuals themselves as well as in the groupings of family or friends who could be mobilized for ongoing support. At this point, it is wise to encourage troubled persons to do as much as possible for themselves. Helpers are partners, in a real sense, with the callers they are trying to assist; they should not do for others what the others can do for themselves.

The next step centers on setting up a concrete plan for action. Arrangements that affect troubled persons should not be made behind their backs, or without including them in the development of the contemplated steps. Thus, if the recommendation is to contact the family doctor, the person should be apprised of this intention and there should be some effort to motivate the individual to agree and to participate willingly in this endeavor.

Not only should the helper emphasize the resources of the person's neighborhood or immediate environment when discussing such a plan by phone, but the counselor should also underscore the positive aspects of the other's personality and immediate life situation. One of the most important things we can do in handling emergencies by phone is to assist others to achieve a more balanced and optimistic perspective about what can be done through the use of available personal and local resources. The helper has a different view of things; this fresh perspective should be shared with people who call us to tell us their troubles on the phone. This should not, of course, be done in a naïve way but rather in a concrete and practical manner. That is a source of hope and help to the distraught caller because it pushes back the walls that seem to be closing in.

One cannot emphasize too strongly the common-sense principle that helpers should never make callers feel worse by emphasizing the negative and harmful aspects of their situation. Counselors who do this can only be harmful, sometimes precipitating serious problems or a negative and dangerous resolution of the crisis at hand. The need to seek out and identify strengths lies at the core of all sensible telephone counseling of others. Telling callers they are worse off than even they think is both dumb and dangerous.

SPECIAL PROBLEMS

What about the confidentiality of discussions conducted by phone? Do the same rules and cautions connected with other counseling apply? As far as the counselor goes, we can answer *yes,* although unless the helper is protected by privilege or professional status, such as is true for members of the clergy, it is not likely that the subject of these conversations will necessarily be legally protected from disclosure in some judicial proceeding. The question of privilege is complex, and state laws have eaten away at the notion of privileged communication to such an extent that helpers, if they are concerned about this aspect of their work, should carefully check local regulations.

The fundamental question that cannot be touched or changed by the law is the confidentiality that is necessarily a part of any trusting relationship. This has been discussed previously (see Chapter VII), and the same warnings about the complexities of making confidentiality explicit (e.g., with clients who attempt to manipulate the helper into it as part of their defensive behavior) apply to all work with others by telephone.

NOTE-TAKING RECORDS

While the nature of emergency work ordinarily precludes the luxury of making extensive notes on the work we do, it remains a sensible practice, even for nonprofessionals. It is a simple matter to jot down the essentials of a critical call, the basics that can so easily be forgotten or distorted. The time, the date, and the substance of the communication should be recorded as a memo to oneself. This is a practical and helpful thing to do, especially if one gets many distress calls, or if one is involved with a person and family members several times over a short period of time. The sequence can easily be forgotten or changed with the passage of even a brief period of time. Many helpers have such busy schedules that such a simple device is absolutely necessary for the sensible management and effectiveness of their work.

CALLERS WHO CAUSE CRISES

The telephone, again because of its special properties, has also become the medium for the expression of conflict and personal inadequacies of startling variety. Thus, obscene callers, to mention but one category, may cause the receivers of such a call—even if they are trained to help others—to react with frustration, disgust, or some other negative feeling. Most of such calls are made to women, and when men answer, the offensive caller ordinarily hangs up. Nonetheless, even male helpers should know something about these problems since they may well be consulted about the difficulties. Indeed, these callers can precipitate crises for women who live alone, and it may be to a male nonprofessional helper that they turn to express their dismay.

These callers often make use of the facilities of hot-line centers that are set up to offer emergency counseling. They know they will get a sympathetic ear, or they hope to, and they may even derive a greater satisfaction out of embarrassing female personnel with their comments, their silence or their descriptions of what they are doing while talking on the phone.

One of the most common of these kinds of calls is that placed by the person who masturbates, using the woman's voice as stimulation. This can be very upsetting for female workers on suicide-prevention lines or for other women engaged in helping work. They report feelings of being used, sexually exploited, and depressed by such callers. If helpers are consulted about such experiences, they should make a clear distinction between providing support and understanding to those women who are victimized, in order to help them understand the nature of their reactions on the one hand, and the need to recommend possible legal and other official intervention on the other. The Telephone Company processes thousands of complaints about such calls every year and has a program for providing relief for customers as well as for cooperating in tracing the offensive individual.

If the helper is called by a person who uses the phone to express himself in this manner, the problem is quite different. Such callers are often poorly developed, extremely isolated persons who, like alcoholics, use denial as a major defense in an attempt to maintain their self-esteem. They ordinarily need sensitive understanding and a referral for long-term treatment.

It is, however, extremely difficult to establish even a minimal relationship with them by phone since they employ that instrument to express their deep personal conflicts. They are sometimes treated brutally when they are apprehended by authorities since there is a perverse and disgusting quality to their activity that sets off a hostile reaction of revengelike proportions in some officials. However, these persons are disturbed and fragile human beings, and counselors, if they can get any kind of foothold of confidence with the caller, should move them toward extended professional help. Counselors should not try to treat these people by phone; rather, they should use any conversation to attempt to arrange a more personal meeting. This, of course, is just what such callers wish to avoid, so helpers should not feel that they have failed if they do not have a high record of successes in working with such persons.

CHRONIC CALLERS

These are people with problems that are different from those of the obscene callers. They can try a helper's patience to the extreme, however, and the task of listening for the person behind the long, complicated, and oft-repeated stories is not an easy one. Public helpers, especially members of the clergy, are extremely vulnerable to chronic callers; they can take up a great deal of a person's time and some sensible effort must be made to manage one's dealings with them without directly rejecting them. Time limits, polite but clear statements that the helper has other obligations: One should not hesitate to use such tactics.

The problem is that many helpers feel guilty if they use such common-sense methods to preserve their schedules, their sanity, and their good humor. Helpers must deal with their own conflicted feelings, however, and not let these generally nonemergency calls take away from the time they should be spending with other people who are more in need of their assistance.

A common type of caller is the person who is already in therapy with some professional. They use the call to elicit sympathy by complaining that their doctor misunderstands or does not treat them well. No nonprofessional helpers should take these as anything but the expression of transference feelings that are arising precisely because these callers are in treatment with someone else.

There is one simple rule that should always be followed: Refer them back to discuss their complaints with the therapists who are supposedly the source of the problem. Do not involve yourself in ill-begotten rescue missions that may violate some other helping relationship and involve you in undermining the work that is someone else's professional responsibility. Even if the emergency helper suspects that there are grounds for dissatisfaction with the professional helper, the proper course is a referral back to that person for a discussion and resolution of whatever difficulties may exist.

For Further Reading

Lester, D., & Brockopp, E. W. (eds.) "Crisis Intervention: Theory, Process and Practice." In *Crisis Intervention and Counseling by Telephone*. Springfield, Ill.: Charles C. Thomas, 1973.

McLuhan, Marshall. *Understanding Media*. New York: New American Library, 1964, Chapter 27, "The Telephone."

Mathis, J. L., and Collins, M. "Progressive phases in group therapy of exhibitionists," *International Journal of Psychotherapy* 20 (1970), pp. 163–69.

Miller, Warren B. "The Telephone in Out-patient Psychotherapy," *American Journal of Psychotherapy* 27:1 (1973), pp. 15–26.

Murray, F. S., and Beran, L. C. "A Survey of Nuisance Calls Received by Males and Females," *Psychological Record* 19 (1968), pp. 107–9.

TWENTY

Even in the Best of Families

THERE are certain garden variety crises that, sooner or later, touch every family, sometimes at its very heart and at other times close enough for everybody to feel the shock waves. Certain experiences, such as death and illness, lie in wait for even the most favored of families, and it seems that ministers, physicians, or lawyers find these problems taking shape and blossoming around them regularly. Such nonprofessional counselors are often the first to know of the problem; they may even have a role in breaking the news or explaining the situation to other family members. Indeed, participating in the resolution of such problems constitutes the daily work of some of these professionals.

What are the most common of these difficulties and how can we provide constructive assistance when they arise?

First, helpers should remember that, while the family is the chief source of support and security for most persons, its very centrality makes any disturbance in it all the more disruptive and psychologically disorganizing. Every family is constantly meeting new challenges and adapting and reorganizing itself in greater or smaller ways in reaction to them. This is the nature of the human situation.

A family that functions reasonably well can handle the routine crises of life without more than supportive assistance from outside. Major problems, however, can tax the adjustive flexibility of any family, and a full-blown crisis—with all the characteristics of any other crisis—may ensue. It is on these occasions that helpers may find that they are already involved and that they need to draw on their knowledge of crisis counseling to intervene effectively.

Often enough, the incident will only be the flower of a problem with roots that are tangled and hidden in the subsurface of family relationships. The illness or the firing will be the focus of feelings and unresolved conflicts that have exerted a steady but unadmitted influence on a family grouping for a number of years.

The helper may well wish to explore these possibilities by standing back from the immediate difficulty to discover what else has been going on. This can be done simply and directly by placing a question, not as an inquisitor but as an understanding and compassionate helper. For example, one might ask "What has been going on in your family lately?" or "Have there been other pressures on all of you over the last year or so?" This helps enormously both in clarifying the setting and in assessing the significance of the present incident. It allows counselors to identify the progression of events and the precipitant of the emergency at hand.

THE THINGS THAT HAPPEN

Death visits every family grouping sooner or later. Its arrival usually touches off a critical period of mourning and readjustment that affects all family members. The survivors must deal with their loss and with the new shape of the family configuration as well as with the problems they will have in adjusting to it. The helper's tasks are centered on assisting the family members to work out their experience of grief and to enter into modified relationships or totally new roles as they attempt to reorient themselves for the future.

Counselors should be aware of the factors, already discussed, that are normally associated with mourning, especially with the largely symbolic manner in which unconscious mourning and readjustment manifest themselves. Even a limited capacity to read the language of the unconscious can make the helper far more effective in aiding people as they attempt to close the gap that death has left in their lives.

There are, however, some practical points that may need attention. The helper, for example, may serve best at the outset of the crisis by helping the main survivor break the news of the death to other family members. Thus, ministers may be the mainstay helpers when sudden or accidental death occurs. They can be present and supportive to the surviving spouse as the children are told and they can assist in rounding up other members or by trying to get some other close relative or friend to play this role if for some reason they cannot accept it themselves.

If the crisis builds up around a family member who is dying, the helper can be the essential mediator of feelings as well as the one who can help family members anticipate the moment of death and its subsequent challenges. These crises are present everywhere. Often, these experiences become full-blown, without the simple but ultimately extraordinarily constructive assistance that can and should be provided by nonprofessional counselors. They have many advantages as they move into such situations. As members of the clergy, physicians or other family advisors, they already know and are known by family members; they occupy an already established position of trust and carry a certain measure of authority—legal, religious, or medical—that can be wisely invoked in the context of the emergency.

In an occurrence as common as death, helpers might not expect that people may need practical advice about very basic questions, such as contacting undertakers, arranging for a burial plot, or deciding on the time and place of religious or memorial services. Every step that we help others to take under the impact of death's visitation is a move forward in resolving the critical nature of the event.

SEPARATION AND MOVING

Death itself may be the Grand Master, but it has less grand manifestations in a number of other common human experiences that trip off our reactions to loss and separation. These "little deaths" are undergone in each separation, whether it is as dramatic as that of spouses who leave each other or the emotional charge that accompanies the exit of the last grown child from home. Similar reactions may surround a family's moving from one place to another. In each of these situations, helpers will find remarkably similar dynamics.

Separation is a pervasive dimension of human experience; it has sharp edges, and some estimate that perhaps as many as half of all psychiatric patients come from families or other social aggregates that are undergoing some separation trauma. What can helpers do to help persons work through these all too familiar problems? Common sense provides some answers. Acknowledging some recapitulation of principles mentioned earlier, we suggest that the helper who is involved close at hand with the stresses of separation may want to do some of the following:

1. Make sure he or she understands the forces that have led to the problem of separation. Use this understanding to assist the parties involved in the situation to sharpen their own appreciation of what has brought them to this moment of decision.

2. Assist those involved to accept further professional consultation about the underlying difficulties. Moving couples on to more intensive counseling without forcing it on them—that is, assisting them to see and

opt for such help—is constructive intervention by the nonprofessional helper.

3. If the separation is not centered on a marital relationship the counselor may be able to alleviate the crisis by bringing about a meeting or reunion between the separated parties. This can occur between family members who have become estranged for whatever reason—such as children and parents now living in different parts of the country—or between friends who have fallen out of sorts with each other. It is a simple step, and if it is carried out without the overzealousness of the insistent do-gooder, it can help enormously in relieving the crisis of separation.

4. Families need support to deal with relocation in strange and unfamiliar settings. It is not unusual for brewing crises, such as relationships between children and parents, to erupt on the occasion of a move to a new neighborhood or city. The stress of separating from friends, relatives, and all that is familiar in one's past is very real. Practical help in both identifying these stresses and putting the affected persons in contact with churches, community agencies, or neighborhood groups is a small but significant way to help the family through the emergency.

MONEY AND WORK CRISES

The psychological significance of a person's work has long been recognized as central to an individual's sense of identity and well-being; it is intimately entwined with self-esteem and the basic unromanticized meaning of human potential. In the same way, a person's wages stand not only for power to purchase goods and services but as a symbol of work's deepest meaning; the scriptural phrase about the laborer being worth his hire echoes in the communal psyche of the race.

Anything, therefore, that disrupts or complicates the work of a man or a woman represents an attack not only on what is profoundly expressive about human nature but also on the core systems of personality through which people understand and comport themselves in relationship to others. Crises centered on financial and work-related matters come to every family, sooner or later, and helpers should have a practical sense of what they can do to be of assistance during a period that has both economic and psychological implications.

Helpers should realize that crises can be touched off by good news as well as bad. At times an individual may react poorly to a significant promotion and salary increase. Success is often more appealing in anticipation than in its arrival. Certain persons, comfortable at a specific level of achievement and responsibility, are thrown for an emotional loss when they are rewarded through advancement to positions of increased accountability and obligation.

Frequently, a fellow worker, executive, or supervisor must manage the individual through the emotionally stressful crisis of either failure or success. Some sense of human nature and a grasp of the pragmatic issues at hand can make them very effective counselors. These are the same requirements for the minister or physician, who may be the first to uncover the problem, especially when it involves financial embarrassment, an altogether too common problem in times when credit is overextended and people are dipping into savings in order to meet their regular bills.

The emotional reactions, which may include a species of immobilizing depression, can be dealt with through basic supportive counseling techniques. The immediate period of the crisis is not the time, as has often been noted, to remake the person's personality. It is rather the occasion to bolster their defenses, to make them stronger, so that they can get through the worst of the challenge. Helpers do not delve into personality dynamics for an ultimate explanation of why the person has generated so much trouble; that can wait for extended help later on. Supportive understanding will suffice while the counselor helps the other to take sensible steps to get things in better order and under improved control.

Thus, for example, nonprofessional helpers should be aware of the assistance that is available through local social-service agencies and should put the individual in touch with a financial advisor retained or recommended by them. There are other practical resources, including specialized groups designed to assist those who are hooked on credit. Membership in these mutual-support groups may be essential for persons who cannot otherwise manage their family finances adequately.

In similar ways, helpers may refer affected persons to local legal assistance. Sometimes families get themselves into financial crunches through their own fault, and lawyers can help them plan, within the parameters of the law, the steps needed to extricate themselves and begin again. On other occasions, persons have financial difficulties, not through their own fault but because they have been victimized by unethical businessmen. This frequently happens to the unlettered or the guileless, who sign up for long-term installment purchases that end up costing them enormous sums of money. Their purchases are often repossessed as well, for they are frequently unaware of even the possibility for recourse. This is the point for practical intervention by the counselor who is in touch with the resources available in the community.

It is a far different situation when a person is experiencing work or financial problems in an isolated and anxiety-producing manner. They are disturbed and yet cannot bring themselves to deal directly with the situation in their work setting. Such conflicts may require helpers to contact their supervisors or associates to mediate the problem in a sensitive but practical manner. Even a contact made by phone to a supervisor may be the successful first step in straightening out a complicated situation. At the very least, some valuable time may be won in which to work through the emotional aspects of the crisis situation.

In the ordinary course of things, the helper is involved in only a brief segment of the readjustment process. This time should be used for emotional support and clarification, for planning and executing practical steps to resolve the tension generated by the work or financial emergency, and for planning follow-up psychological and other appropriate counseling to help the person deal with deeper personal problems and design more acceptable economic practices for the future.

FAMILY FIGHTS

These are a fact of life, and nonprofessional counselors, be they teachers, members of the clergy, physicians, lawyers, or police, are all too familiar with them. They happen all the time, and the nonprofessional is almost always the one who gets called into the middle of the ring to serve as referee. What can helpers do, both to avoid being hit by stray blows and to assist the parties to make peace and take some constructive steps toward dealing with underlying problems?

Short-term explosive family crises are not the occasion for profound, uncovering efforts at psychotherapy. We may have to settle for very modest goals when we find ourselves involved in these tense situations. What we do may have to be calibrated to the maturity of the parties involved. After all, in a family fight we frequently see the real psychological age-level of the participants revealed in the nature and style of the encounter. Some are hardly more than children, and their expectations and demands reflect their poor development. More-adult persons can have disagreements as well, but they also have the capacity to observe themselves and to put things right in a much more grown-up way. Deciding the level of development is the first challenge faced by the would-be counselor.

Secondly, helpers should not hesitate to assume an active posture; they can ask questions and move into the issues, even the most sensitive ones, without unnecessary caution. They can do this in informal settings, such as police stations and emergency rooms, where a key act in the family drama may be being played out, or in more formalized places, such as an office or other neutral location. They can talk to affected family members as a group, taking advantage of their nonprofessional relationship, to define briefly the central issues that have brought about the crisis.

This is not to suggest elaborate psychological probing as much as it is to recognize the advantage the family confidant—the priest, the doctor—possesses at such moments. Without making the entangled parties defensive they may be able to speak clearly about the long-standing pressures and unresolved issues that flash periodically into emergency problems. The actual time of the crisis offers a valuable period in which to examine the causes by raising the general question: "What do you have to look at together in order to avoid these blow-ups?" A question framed along these lines can set the theme for subsequent counseling assistance as well as help the couple get through the current manifestation of their problem.

A helper with some skill can use this difficult interval constructively by helping family members to see just how they interact to create the final crisis situation. One can often identify the "scapegoating" process in a family, in which all the difficulties are heaped on one member; this defensive technique relieves the family's need to explore deeper problems. But they cannot make these deeper explorations, or even imagine that they should, unless they are helped to see what they are doing with and to each other. Nor is it very complicated to see how parents may be keeping a child in a dependent position—e.g., taking care of an unemployed adult son—in order to reap certain gratifications from this, even at the risk of periodic explosions through the son's acting-out behavior.

Helpers who are familiar with the dynamics of the situation can usually read them accurately and help family members to achieve at least minimal insight into the disagreement and fights that seem to repeat themselves over and over again. Eventually, if permanent progress is to be made, the family members will have to get long-term help to get to the basic dynamics of these cycles. The occasion of a blow-up allows the helper to point them in the right direction.

The same general notions apply to the critical phase in marital estrangement. In the short-term opportunity of the explosive incident, helpers can not only offer support appropriate to the maturity of the beleaguered participants but also frame the emergency with larger meaning and identify issues that should be dealt with in follow-up counseling. The helper should relieve the immediate tension of the crisis, if possible, but not allow the couple, or the family grouping, to slip back into the same battle-ready positions that they will assume if they don't get further assistance.

TWENTY ONE

The Ill and the Injured

A torrent of literature has swept across America during the last generation on the subject of death and dying. Workshops, lectures, and discussion groups have centered on the insights about the journey of the terminally ill toward death. The hospice movement, gaining new momentum in the Eighties, recognizes the need for an enlightened and sensitive environment for those facing the certainty of death.

And yet the nonprofessional counselor may find that the crisis of death seldom unfolds across a comfortable period of time, that people are killed in accidents even before surprise can register on their faces, and that illnesses can be insidious in their onset, making their fatal presence known when there is hardly time left for recollection or preparation. A subset of this may be found in the way in which unexpected illnesses, such as heart attacks and strokes, can shatter lives without warning, scattering the pieces of a once unquestioned adjustment in such a fashion that they cannot be fit together again.

The fact of illness and death that confronts the crisis worker is frequently hideous in aspect, as shocking to the helper as to the victims and their relatives. What can counselors do in these circumstances, which, however they may vary, possess such a violent and intrusive core?

THE SUDDENLY ILL

Excitement and confusion are the environment for those incidents in which persons, confident and unknowing in the morning, find themselves stricken in some unpredictable manner during the day. These include persons who suffer accidents, such as car or industrial mishaps, or those who have heart attacks or strokes, as well as individuals who find that their routine physical check-up turns out not to be routine at all in its findings. In the latter group one must also include those for whom, in a real sense, the jury is still out while tests and other examinations are conducted because of some ominous finding in a medical examination.

These are the problems that people dread and wish not to think about; they are the crises faced by physicians, members of the clergy, and other nonprofessional counselors many times every week.

The first common-sense rule, echoed in clichés like "stand back" or "give them air," is the priority of getting adequate medical attention before achieving any other goal. One may be more inclined to handle the emotional aspects of the problem, but this is surely secondary when one is involved in an obvious physical emergency. All efforts should go into beginning the emergency medical treatment. Also, those nearby should be kept from interfering or meddling or giving amateur assistance.

A helper with a clear head and a willingness to take over can quickly organize the efforts, shaping a purposeful move toward proper medical aid out of the confusion of the incident. Just as a *triage* office has the responsibility for designating priorities in an emergency room at the time of mass disaster, so the crisis counselor, on a lesser scale, can orchestrate the responses at the scene of an accident or at the sudden onset of serious illness.

The injured or afflicted person may well be conscious throughout the event, whether it is an accident or a physical attack. Anxiety about what is happening can grip the person, compromising his or her condition severely. Obviously, helpers want to avoid doing anything that would deepen that anxiety even while they are arranging for help. One can handle it best by telling the injured or sick person who you are, what you are doing, and if arrangements are far enough advanced, what the next move will be, as, for example, to an emergency room or a doctor's office.

As events move along, it is important to avoid making pessimistic observations about the individual's condition, even if he or she seems to be unconscious. Saying how bad things are, or how much worse they might get, is no help to anyone during such a critical time.

It is important to tell the person that, you will contact family members, if this has not already been taken care of. This is often comforting to the afflicted person, who feels alone in the face of a new and extremely threatening experience. The next step, of course, is to do this, simply and directly, telling the nearest relative what has happened, what is being done, and where the family should go to see the patient, with, if possible, some plan to meet them when family members arrive.

If the crisis worker remains with the victim during the time of transport to the emergency room or after arrival, he or she can help the afflicted person to cope with the strangeness and confusion of the emergency. One can, for example, explain simply where the ambulance is going, the nature of the emergency room or the temporary shelter, or whatever else is appropriate to the concrete circumstances. Assisting the person to understand the map of the suddenly changed world can be very supportive.

BUT WHAT DO YOU SAY?

Common sense or prudence should again prevail in handling this difficult but all too familiar challenge. Uncomfortable silence delivers its own message and ordinarily increases anxiety for the patient at the same time. Bluff reassurances don't work for persons who understand that something of major proportions has befallen them. Sensible honesty, as always, is the best policy.

Here the counselor's sensitivity to human issues becomes quite important again. We can give a brief, truthful description without using words or phrases that are intrinsically shocking. We can acknowledge the seriousness of the occurrence without aggravating it by some woeful judgment about the outcome. Helpers want to help preserve the injured person's will to remain engaged with life; they do not wish, by word or gesture, to snuff out that essential ingredient to recovery, hope itself.

Study after study has revealed that those patients whose hope is destroyed also do worst in dealing with their injuries or other illness. It is the vital stuff, the "right stuff" indeed, at a time of physical danger, and the emergency worker may be the key person to nourish it by sensibly and honestly responding to questions about the nature of the difficulty.

Suppose the person asks directly whether he or she is dying? This is by no means an unusual question, and it is not one to which we should respond with a lie or a major distortion of the facts. If, in fact, the person is dying, one can say "Yes," but not in the tones of a tolling bell. That reply can be given as a realistic human response that meets the perception of the individual without crushing out hope. It can be uttered in the tones of one who is sticking with the patient or the victim and who will remain there to fight it out as long as possible.

There are situations, of course, in which persons are not in danger of death, despite the seriousness of their injuries. They need to be told the truth simply and directly as well, again with the importance of hope underscored and the determination to fight the problem through reinforced.

It is not unusual for a person to be concerned about others who may have been in the same accident, fire, or other disaster. A person may want to know the condition of spouse or children. While the person is under tremendous pressure from his or her own physical problems, along with the complicating anxiety, discretion is very important. This is just another word for common sense because, although the truth is always reliable, the truth, especially a brutal and discouraging truth, need not be told all at once or, for that matter, immediately.

Piling a devastating truth on top of a gruesome reality may be enough to send the patient into shock, thus decreasing chances for survival. Crisis workers may have to feel their way through such situations, keeping good sense as their best guide to their interventions.

THE PEOPLE WHO RESIST

Human beings are intensely interesting and various in their responses to sudden physical problems. Some resent it, preferring to ignore or strangely challenge death, even when they are faced with absolute proof about the seriousness of their condition. Some may refuse to believe it or reject the idea of going to an emergency room or some place for diagnosis or treatment.

The task of emergency workers is to impress on such individuals the seriousness of their condition. This should not be done through some near-violent confrontation but, again, through a calm and purposeful explanation of the true state of affairs. One cannot, of course, convince the terminally stubborn to face the facts about their health or their need for an operation or some other form of treatment, but even with the reluctant, one can expect to make some headway through the use of the truth about the situation and the consequences if no action is taken.

Common sense also dictates that we do the practical thing in urgent situations. For example, if a surgical procedure is required and the individual is unconscious, the crisis counselor can contact a family member for the necessary agreement to the operation. There are many such decisions that the physician and others who are constantly involved in such matters must deal with on a regular basis. Nonmedical helpers can be of assistance to them by getting them in touch with responsible relatives at the time of the crisis. A counselor should not, of course, usurp a responsibility that properly belongs to a medical person. Doctors and nurses or paramedics should be consulted before making any moves that require their advice or consultation.

Perhaps the best preparation for such crises of illness or accident is to be prepared for surprises. People sometimes do not react the way a textbook predicts that they will. There may be elements in the situation that need delicate handling or a request to inform nonfamily members about the incident. It is impossible to be sure of the exact nature of the potential occurrences, but one should be ready for surprises in some form or other. Anticipating one's own uneasiness or uncertainty allows one to deal even with the most unexpected developments in a calm and confident manner.

SUPPOSE A CHILD IS HURT

The same common-sense principles for responding to adults apply when a child is injured. Naturally, one must be aware of the extraordinary pressures generated by such an incident and make some allowances. For example, many authorities believe that it is wise and humane to allow the parents to stay near the child, perhaps even in the hospital treatment room. This allays the anxiety that both parents and children share in such circumstances. Separation may only heighten the anxiety and make things worse for all concerned.

RESPONDING TO RELATIVES

One of the major responsibilities of the crisis counselor is the sensitive and humane dealing with relatives of the injured or dying person. The application of a few simple principles can make this task much less stressful for all concerned. Again, this is a matter of common sense and mature human feeling rather than hard and fast regulations.

Perhaps the first thing helpers should realize is that although they have an indispensable role to play, they cannot and should not take over responsibilities that belong to the medical personnel at an accident scene or in a hospital setting. The physician should be allowed to communicate all relevant information about the injured person's condition, including, if it is the case, his or her death. Relatives feel better about the care of the person if a physician communicates with them; it reassures them, eliminating questions about whether adequate medical care was delivered. Crisis counselors should be ready to take over once the information has been given to the relatives.

The latter may well be in a state of shock and may be confused or uncertain about what steps can or should be taken next. They will need the firm and purposeful direction of a helper who can assist them in understanding and undertaking the many tasks that lie before the family at a time of such difficulty. It is possible that one or the other was also in the accident that caused the serious injury; these should be referred for physical examination even if they seem reluctant to accept the idea. If the helper is assisting at the location of the accident, he or she should see to it that if it is at all possible a relative accompany the injured person in the ambulance on the way to the hospital.

If the family has been notified by phone of an accident or injury affecting a family member, they should also be given clear instructions about where to go and whom to look for on arrival at the hospital or other site of treatment. Counselors should arrange to meet them at this place and also see to it that there is a place of privacy, a small room or an office, in which they can meet the doctor or await news of the patient's condition. Breaking news to people in hallways or other public places creates an awkward and emotionally stressful situation that can ordinarily be avoided with a little sensible planning. In many hospitals, facilities have been designed to insure some of the psychologically necessary privacy during these difficult times.

Workers should coordinate their activities so that they do not interfere with those of the medical personnel but rather assist them in managing the family's needs. Thus, it is the physician or nurses, not the counselor, who give permission to see the patient, if at all possible, before surgery, or, sadly, in death itself. Physicians should understand that such powerful experiences should be neither denied to relatives nor diluted on the basis of the theory that this will make them more bearable. Relatives should not be swiftly sedated, for example, after they receive news of the death of a loved one. Suppression of emotional reaction is neither wise nor healthy. People should be allowed to feel what they are going through; counselors are there not to soften the experience but to stand with people as they enter into it.

Spouses, for example, should be allowed to be with their wives or husbands at the moment of death. As Kübler-Ross has written: "When a patient is close to death, do not send the relatives out of the room 'to spare them.' Clinical experience shows that this action only adds to their grief and does not make it easier later on. A wife who holds her husband's hand when he takes his last breath feels better than if she had retreated to a lonely hallway or a cold waiting room until she is notified it is all over" ("Dying Persons and Their Families," *Emergency Psychiatric Care*).

Most doctors understand this, of course, but facing death as often as they do, they may have to remind themselves that individual death is a solemn and irreplaceable experience—a singular and necessary event— for the loved ones of the deceased. Often relatives wish to see the body after death has occurred. This should always be allowed, and helpers should not, out of false sympathy, try to prevent this viewing. It is important psychologically in ways that we do not fully understand; it seems to allow the mourning process to proceed. Such was observed, for example, when the remains of servicemen who had been missing in action were returned after the end of the Vietnam War. The relatives who opted to view them seemed to be helped by the experience. It is as if the chance to somehow touch the deceased allows an important psychological passage to be made.

No Need to Rush

Crisis workers should feel no pressure to get on to or back to something else. It is better not to do this kind of work than it is to do it with a consciousness of time that is more appropriate to an air-traffic controller than to an emergency worker. People need time, and they need somebody to be with them as they sort out the event and face and deal with the many practical decisions that may confront them at such times.

Helpers should be ready for outbursts of anger or sorrow, which are perfectly natural and predictable. It is commonplace for people to want to blame somebody else—alas, it is often the doctor—for the condition of their loved one. Such displacement of feeling is often without any basis in fact; it is just the channel for the survivors' own unresolved feelings at the time of death. So, too, counselors can expect some of the other fruits of the ambivalence that, to one degree or another, we all share about those who are close to us. People may express regret, rage, and a number of other emotions. We should not try to argue about these feelings or their motivation. Grief is a human but not a logical process.

Other Questions

In the case of sudden and unexplained death, the law may require an autopsy. The physician may, in some circumstances, feel that this is necessary as well. While voluntary cooperation after enlightened explanation works more often than not for the latter, legal requirements demand acceptance of plans for an autopsy. This may have to be explained sensitively to family members by the physician who is involved. Counselors cannot take the physician's role, but they can provide support and understanding at the time such a decision is made. Once again, common-sense understanding is the surest ally of the helper.

An alert counselor may become aware that some member of the surviving relatives is experiencing a reaction that goes beyond the normal grief responses. The individual who seems not to react at all, expresses no emotion, or evinces the symptoms of depression may need special care. In some situations, such persons need to be treated both with supportive counseling and continued care. If, for example, a survivor speaks of suicide and shows some of the danger signs of carrying out a plan, some prompt action should be taken, including the possibility of at least temporary hospitalization.

Follow-up support is one of the great gifts that even amateur counselors can quite effectively bestow on those who have been through such emergency problems. The pastor who calls up every few days, the doctor who takes the time to keep in touch: These play a wonderful healing role in the lives of those who grieve and mourn.

For Further Reading

Caine, Lynn. *Widow*. New York: William Morrow, 1974.

Hinton, John. *Dying*. New York: Penguin, 1967.

Kubler-Ross, Elisabeth. *Questions and Answers on Death and Dying*. New York: Macmillan & Co., 1974.

Resnik, H.; Ruben, H.; and Ruben, eds. "Dying Persons and Their Families," *Emergency Psychiatric Care*. Bowie, Maryland: The Charles Press Publishers, Inc., 1957, p. 148.

TWENTY TWO

Crises for the Counselor

THE stress of emergency counseling work is enormous, and no helper is immune from its effects. Indeed, those professionals who find that their ordinary work leads them regularly into situations in which they deal with intensely critical incidents need to examine their lives and their schedules periodically for the sake of their own mental health and the continued good quality of their involvement with others.

It is not just a question of a check-up for the sake of the helper. That is, of course, important in itself, but its significance is increased in view of the impact a weary or burnt-out helper can have on those who need assistance. Ethical considerations are also relevant since counselors have a real responsibility for using themselves well—and, therefore, for keeping themselves in good condition—for the sake of others.

People who become members of the clergy, or who coach, teach, or give of themselves in some service occupation that touches on the emergencies of life have a real desire to be helpful to others. For some, this may even be a need whose nature they do not understand, much less admit to themselves.

The chief reward of their intervention in difficult circumstances, such as those that normally surround crises, arises from assisting others. They experience compassion and sympathy, profoundly important emotions, but also feelings that can draw them into confusing involvements and drive them on to help others almost relentlessly in order to avoid feeling guilty. Such helpers can be very hard on themselves as well as endlessly troubled about whether they have done enough, or whether they should increase their follow-up in certain cases. Their very feeling for the woes of others can, in other words, be the source of many of the stresses that they encounter in emergency work.

One thing that such highly motivated persons should not tax themselves with is feeling bad because they at times feel weighed down by the difficult emergency work that comes in the course of their other professional endeavors. It is perfectly acceptable to be worn down; stress is neither an infectious disease nor a sinful indulgence. It is a by-product of close work with people who hurt, and it should be expected, even actively anticipated, in the lives of sensible helpers. They should learn to identify the stresses to which they are particularly susceptible, to monitor them sensibly, and to take common-sense steps to keep themselves in good balance. Admitting that major problems can get to us, can eat away at our resistance, is a first and indispensable step toward good management of our crisis work.

A JOB WHERE THINGS GO WRONG

By definition, crises are situations in which things have gone very wrong, episodes in which the events of life have bunched up, like cars in a chain-reaction accident, often at the worst possible time for everyone concerned. Philosophically, emergency workers should not feel, then, that they can ever provide a response which will successfully make up for an event that is, by nature, a gaping wound. We should not expect that we can make up for death and loss, for accident and separation.

As counselors, we are essentially doing our best not to make things worse and to take the steps that will get the flow of life moving again and allow, where necessary, the process of healing to get started. We should not be surprised if despite our best efforts and our hard study, things do not work out the way we would like. Crises surprise and unbalance not only those who are directly affected by them but also those of us who help others in these emergency situations. We must learn to accept human resolutions to these difficult and anguishing events. Performing miracles is not the calling of the crisis helper.

The needs and feelings of emergency workers are quite important since they are part of the ingredients in the effort to establish order and priorities in complex problems. Many of the things that emergency workers would like to have work—even the machines in emergency rooms—sometimes just do not work as they are supposed to.

Perhaps a Murphy's Law of expectation is needed for anybody doing crisis work. Things often have a life of their own at the time of a crisis, and we have to be ready, like generals in a battle, to move to fall-back positions, or to try the next best thing, or just to use common sense, when the suggestions from workshops, courses, or even books like this one, simply don't work out perfectly in practice. The crisis worker needs, however, to preserve one thing in the midst of the chaos of disintegrating events: a sense of presence that enables the best employment of good judgment in assessing and putting order into things. The crisis worker who cannot be philosophical finds that the stress of emergency work becomes impacted and self-defeating.

THAT'S EASY TO SAY

Because presence—and the calmness and sense of knowing what to do that goes with it—is so essential in an emergency, helpers should search out their own reactions, anticipating if they can, how they will behave in a variety of critical events. Such an effort to sound out one's feelings in advance is not very difficult; all a person has to do is use his or her imagination in structuring the impact of specific problems on themselves. Just as realistic run-throughs of disasters help hospital staffs to learn about their own weaknesses and strengths so that they can manage themselves better when the real thing hits, so the helper, even the isolated individual without the luxury of a rehearsal or the support of other team members, can think ahead and monitor potential reactions in order to be able to deal with them more maturely when a true crisis arrives. This does not require melodramatics—nor does it demand a screenwriter's creativity—because it is built on something that most helpers already possess: a capacity to put themselves in other people's shoes.

If helpers are not accustomed to reflecting on their own emotional experiences, they are missing a very important opportunity to solidify their own sense of presence. The only things that can trip up emergency workers at moments of real trial are the aspects of themselves which they have failed to attend to. What they don't know about themselves does, in fact, harm them. While the use of denial is absolutely necessary during certain aspects of crisis work—as, for example, if one must deal with seriously wounded people or help recover bodies after an accident—it is not a good defensive posture to use in the ordinary course of life.

Since this book is addressed to counselors who are neither professional therapists nor professional crisis workers, it is all the more important that they have a good working knowledge of their own affective lives. The most basic principle of sound mental health recommends that we be able to correctly name the experiences we have, acknowledging as consciously as possible the nature of our feelings, even if they are not the kind we would prefer ideally to have. Control of our emotions depends not on looking away from them but on facing them without fear and learning to live at peace with them while we grow toward more mature behavior.

Becoming an adult is a life-long task, and emergency workers should not feel ashamed of themselves if they discover that they still have some growing up to do. Developing what is described as an "observing self" is indispensable for the crisis worker, who must be able to be involved in very serious human problems while at the same time monitoring his or her reactions. This latter should not be done in the manner of a field marshall reviewing the troops but in the way an understanding friend would listen to our troubles, without rancor or unnecessarily harsh judgment.

A confident presence is the outcome of our being able to observe and live with our growing selves. This is, at one and the same time, the solid anchor of our crisis work and the strongest inner support we can enjoy in the wearing work of helping in emergencies.

A LOOK AT OTHERS

Our own strength is fortified even more when we are able to share our crisis responsibilities with others. This is the case when we are members of a team, as when one works with a group of fellow pastors or teachers during a particular emergency. The group also brings stresses since it necessarily involves us with different viewpoints and different approaches. The counselor who maintains good mental health also improves the functioning of the team; such a person can also assist coworkers immeasurably by bringing the same kind of openness and understanding to them that he or she brings to himself or herself.

The needs and feelings of others are supremely important. The person who knows how to lead possesses an instinctive feel for this and makes room for the contributions that others can make even though these may not come from specialized training. Oftentimes during emergencies the persons who know the area and the people who live there can sense and predict reactions with much greater certainty than the psychological experts. If we are prepared to allow each person who is cooperating in the crisis to contribute at least a portion of what their special talent is, the stress on the group will be notably lessened. The outcome of the intervention will also be improved.

It is obviously helpful if a group of workers who collaborate even on an irregular basis can get together to explore their feelings and to discuss the stresses that they encounter in the course of their crisis interventions. Such discussions allow the team to anticipate future problems and to solidify their sense of competence.

THINGS TO KNOW ABOUT ONESELF

In order to successfully manage our own adjustment we have to make use of the information that the "observing self" gives to us. People who choose helping professions enjoy the strength of their capacity for sympathy with others. The other side of this, however, may be seen in their own sensitivity to evidences of criticism, dislike, or a lack of appreciation.

Nonprofessional counselors, especially members of the clergy and those in the teaching profession, like being liked. Their work would otherwise be intolerable. Crises frequently plunge them into situations in which they are going to become the objects of the displaced rage and anger of the affected people. Some knowledge of the transference phenomenon tells helpers that these strong feelings are not directed at them personally but that they are receiving them because they are the available targets for some of the strong reactions that occur at times of emergency.

It is all very well in the abstract to tell helpers that they need not take these reactions personally. It is extremely difficult, however, for them to believe this when they are on the receiving end of a distraught person's wrath. Here, again, helpers must view this experience from the vantage point of the observer within themselves; from this perspective they can separate the generalized hostility at the inequity of the universe from any feelings that might have a truly personal reference for them.

People who cannot handle such misplaced hostility might better avoid certain emergency work in which it is bound to make an appearance. The capacity to accept these wails that rise up like those of the biblical Rachel after suffering and death is essential for the person who is going to maintain a balance, be a source of organization, and provide strength and comfort to the afflicted. Helpers should explore in advance their own ability to stand up under what seem to be fierce attacks. Being able to understand these as not directed at them personally protects them and enables them to function constructively.

It hardly needs to be noted that crisis workers should avoid giving troubled people any realistic grounds for angry reactions. Helpers usually strive to avoid being abrasive or indiscreet, so this is generally not a major source of difficulty. Some helpers, however, having had a little training or having done a little reading in psychology, may unwisely use some technique such as confrontation; or they may place intrusive questions that can bring a deserved reaction of anger from those they wish to help.

Another common problem for helpers centers on their capacity to accept failure in working with others. They want things to work out for other people; they are all in favor of happy endings. Helpers who need success will be bitterly disappointed when they find out that failure, at least in some partial way, is intrinsic to almost every one of their efforts to help others. Sometimes this sense of failure stems from the unreasonable expectations they make on themselves. Before they can function effectively in crises, they must come to terms in an understanding way with their own perfectionistic tendencies. In any helping occupation, even highly trained persons can only do their best. Helpers who cannot accept compromise with perfection only cripple themselves and lessen their effectiveness.

Second cousin to all these, and most menacing of all reactions for some helpers, is the experience of rejection. Few things hurt helpers more than the active rejection of their most sincere efforts to help others. Sometimes this rejection is as biting as the breaking of a love affair because the helper is totally vulnerable in the situation and can become the prey of the crisis victim, even as the lover can be the prey of the beloved. There is no way to eliminate this risk from the helping occupations.

Obviously, workers who build their self-esteem on the emotional rewards of assisting others will be far more vulnerable to rejection than persons who have a solid sense of themselves and their own powers independent of the crisis work they do. The best preparation for facing rejection and the kindred hazards of working at close hand with the injured and the bereaved is to come to terms with ourselves outside these circumstances. Our self-esteem and our other emotional needs cannot feed from the springs of crisis situations. We do not build our personal lives on the emotional uplift or impact of being involved in critical occurrences. We are not carrion-lovers involving ourselves in human disaster to feast on the dependent and the emotionally injured. Good mental health is evidenced in the maturity of individuals who are secure in themselves and who have in their personal lives sources of emotional sustenance that are independent of their work.

COMMON-SENSE IDEAS

Crisis workers who are not professional counselors should always perceive this specialized work as incidental to their main activity in life. If they notice through self-observation that the proportion of emergency work to the tasks of their regular jobs is shifting notably, they must ask themselves why, and make some adjustment to get things back in proper order again. There is, after all, something attractive as well as something forbidding about crisis situations.

When our day to day activities are routine, as they often are for teachers, doctors and the clergy, the summons to an emergency can confer a new sense of purpose and excitement, which can be heady seasoning in an otherwise bland round of activities. Crises should remain the exception in the lives of most professionals. They should not indulge their "rescue fantasies" or their need to help in such a way that they seek out crises instead of responding to them when they occur.

Helpers must make sure that they have a proper diet and get enough rest and exercise if they wish to function effectively when the stresses of a crisis grip them. It is strange, to note, however, how many professional people do not attend sensibly to these basics of a well-organized and healthy life; some also fail to schedule their day's activities or define their availability for emergency work in a way that guarantees a healthy balance of activity in their lives. Any helpers who find that they need to be "on call" or who seem to need a "beeper" as a sign of their commitment or indispensability should also reexamine their priorities.

Perhaps the most helpful thing for helpers is to seek out on a regular basis the supervision of a professional person who has an understanding of counseling and its application to emergency work. While discussion of our stresses with a colleague or a friend may be profitable, there is no activity that better helps us to view our own work from a mature perspective than such supervision. Sometimes a group of clergy or teachers can join together in paying a professional supervisor to go over their work at a regular time each week or each month.

Helpers learn to look at themselves from the viewpoint of their mature observing-self much more readily when they are assisted by the sage observations of a good supervisor. This enables them to keep their own emotional needs in order and to deal constructively with the stresses that attend their work in times of crisis. It also enables them to perfect their skills, to learn what has gone wrong in their work, and to continue to grow in harmonizing their major professional activity with the demands of the emergencies that will continue to occur regularly.

For Further Reading

APA, "Ethical Standards of Psychologists." Washington, DC: American Psychological Association, Inc., 1977.

Arieti, Silvano. *The Intraphysic Self.* New York: Basic Books, 1967.

Benjamin, Alfred. *The Helping Interview,* 2nd ed. New York: Houghton-Mifflin, 1974.

Blocher, D. (ed.) *Developmental Counseling,* 2nd ed. The Ronald Press Company, 1974.

Brammer, Lawrence M. *The Helping Relationship.* Englewood Cliffs, N.J.: Prentice-Hall, Inc., 1973.

Brammer, Lawrence M., and Shostrom, E. *Therapeutic Psychology.* Englewood Cliffs, N.J.: Prentice-Hall, Inc., 1968.

Egan, Gerard. *The Skilled Helper.* Belmont, California: Wadsworth Publishing Company, Inc., 1975.

Erikson, Erik H. *Childhood and Society.* New York: W.W. Norton & Company, Inc., 1963.

Jourard, Sidney M. *The Transparent Self.* New York: Van Nostrand Reinhold Company, 1971.

Luft, Joseph. *Of Human Interaction.* Joseph Luft, 1968.

NASW, "Code of Ethics," New York: National Association of Social Workers, 1960, 1967.

Patterson, C. H. "A Model for Counseling and Other Facilitative Human Relationships." In *Counseling and Guidance in the Twentieth Century* (W. Van Hoose, and J. J. Pietrofesa, eds.). New York: Houghton-Mifflin, 1970.

Rogers, Carl R. *Client-Centered Therapy.* Carl R. Rogers, 1957.

———. *On Becoming A Person.* Carl R. Rogers, 1961.